WHERE
WE GOT
THE BIBLE

OUR DEBT TO THE CATHOLIC CHURCH

WHERE WE GOT THE BIBLE

OUR DEBT TO THE CATHOLIC CHURCH

By

Rt. Rev. Henry G. Graham

Author of *Hindrances to Conversion*, etc.

> "All scripture, inspired of God, is prof-
> itable to teach, to reprove, to correct, to
> instruct in justice, that the man of God
> may be perfect, furnished to every good
> work."   —2 Timothy 3:16-17

TAN BOOKS AND PUBLISHERS

Nihil Obstat et Imprimatur
JOANNES RITCHIE, *Vic. Gen.*
Glasguae

Originally published by B. Herder Book Co., St. Louis, Missouri. Reprinted in 1977 by TAN Books and Publishers, Inc. Retypeset and republished by TAN in 2004.

ISBN: 978-0-89555-796-4

History of the First 31 Printings

1st Printing, 1911	*17th Printing, 1977*
2nd Printing (Revised), 1924	*18th Printing, 1979*
3rd Printing, 1927	*19th Printing, 1981*
4th Printing, 1931	*20th Printing, 1985*
5th Printing, 1932	*21st Printing, 1986*
6th Printing, 1934	*22nd Printing, 1987*
7th Printing, 1935	*23rd Printing, 1989*
8th Printing, 1936	*24th Printing, 1992*
9th Printing (Revised), 1939	*25th Printing, 1994*
10th Printing, 1940	*26th Printing, 1997*
11th Printing, 1948	*27th Printing, 1997*
12th Printing, 1950	*28th Printing, 1999*
13th Printing, 1952	*29th Printing, 2001*
14th Printing, 1955	*30th Printing (Retypeset), 2004*
15th Printing, 1957	*31st Printing, 2007*
16th Printing, 1960	*32nd Printing, 2009*

Printed and bound in the United States of America.

TAN BOOKS AND PUBLISHERS

2004

Dedicated to
All Lovers of the Written Word of God,
"in which are certain things hard to be understood, which the unlearned and unstable wrest, as they do also the other scriptures, to their own destruction."   —*2 Peter* 3:16

"I would not believe the Gospel unless moved thereto by the authority of the Church."

> —St. Augustine
> (*Contra Epis. Manich.,
> Fund.*, n. 6)

Preface to the First Edition

THIS little book about the Bible grew out of lectures which the writer delivered on the subject to mixed audiences. The lectures were afterwards expanded, and appeared in a series of articles in the Catholic press 1908-9, and are now with slight alterations reprinted. Their origin will sufficiently account for the colloquial style employed throughout.

There is, therefore, no pretense either of profound scholarship or of eloquent language; all that is attempted is a popular and, as far as possible, accurate exposition along familiar lines of the Catholic claim historically in regard to the Bible. It is candidly controversial without, however, let us hope, being uncharitable or unfair.

Friends had more than once suggested the reissue of the articles; and it appeared to the writer that at last the proper moment for it had come when the Protestant world is jubilating over the Tercentenary of the Authorized Version. Amidst the flood of literature on the subject of the Bible, it seemed but right that some statement, however plain and simple, should be set forth from the Catholic side, with the object of bringing home to the average mind the debt that Britain, in common with the rest of Christendom, owes to the Catholic Church in this connection. Probably the motive of the present publication will be best understood by a perusal of the following letter from the writer which appeared in the *Glasgow Herald*, 18th of March, 1911:

The Bible Centenary and
the Catholic Church

Amid the general jubilation over the three hundredth anniversary of the appearance of King James's version of the Bible, I think it would be a pity if we did not make mention of that great Church to which, under God, we owe our possession of the sacred Scriptures—I mean of course, the Roman Catholic Church. Without striking one single jarring note, I hope, in the universal chorus, yet I feel it would be rather ungenerous, and indeed historically unjust, did we not turn our eyes at least in passing to that venerable figure standing in the background surveying our celebrations, and, as it were, saying, "Rejoice over it, but remember it was from me you got it." As a Scotsman, who cannot forget that it is the Bible that has made Scotland largely what she is today, I yield to no one in veneration of the inspired Scriptures and in admiration of the incomparably beautiful Authorized Version. Still, honor to whom honor. We shall only be awarding a just meed of praise and gratitude if we frankly and thankfully recognize that it is to a council (or councils) of the R.C. Church that we owe the collection of the separate books into our present

Canon of the New Testament, and that to the loving care and devoted labor of the monks and scholars of that Church all through the ages we are indebted, not only for the multiplication and distribution of the sacred volume among the faithful when as yet no printing press existed, but even for the preservation of the Book from corruption and destruction. It is, then, undoubtedly true to say that, in the present order of Providence, it is owing to the Roman Catholic Church that we have a Bible at all. And no one will be a bit the worse Christian and Bible-lover if he remembers, this notable year, that it is to the Mother Church of Christendom he must look if he would behold the real preserver, defender, and transmitter of the "Word that endureth for ever."

HENRY GREY GRAHAM

Contents

WHERE
WE GOT
THE BIBLE

OUR DEBT TO THE CATHOLIC CHURCH

∽ Introduction ∽

Rome Hates the Bible?

IF all were true that is alleged against the Catholic Church in her treatment of Holy Scripture, then the proper title of these papers should be not "How we got", but "How we have not got the Bible". The common and received opinion about the matter among non-Catholics in Britain, for the most part, has been that Rome hates the Bible—that she has done all she could to destroy it—that in all countries where she has held power and sway she has kept the Bible from the hands of the people—has taken it and burned it whenever she found anyone reading it. Or if she cannot altogether prevent its publication or its perusal, at least she renders it as nearly useless as possible by sealing it up in a dead language which the majority of people can neither read nor understand. And all this she does, so we are told, because she knows that her doctrines are absolutely opposed to and contradicted by the letter of God's written Word. She holds and propagates dogmas and traditions which could not stand one moment's examination if exposed to the searching light of Holy Scripture. As a matter of fact, is it not known to everybody that, when the Bible was for the first time brought to the light

1

and printed and put into the people's hands in the
sixteenth century, suddenly there was a great
revolt against the Roman Church—there was a
glorious Reformation? The people eagerly gazing
upon the open Bible, saw they had been befooled
and hoodwinked and been taught to hold "for doctrines the commandments of men," and forthwith
throwing off the fetters and emancipating themselves from the bondage of Romanism, they
embraced the pure truth of the Word of God as set
forth in Protestantism and Protestant Bibles.

Is not this the tale that history tells about
Rome? Has she not always waged a cruel and
relentless war against the Holy Book—issued
prohibitions and framed decrees against reading
it or having it in the house—sometimes even in
her deadly hatred going to the length of making
bonfires of heaps of Old and New Testaments, as
Tunstall, Bishop of London, did to William Tyndale's? Has she not burned at the stake, or at
least banished from their home and country, ser-
vants of the Lord like John Wycliffe and William
Tyndale for no other crime than that of translating and printing and putting into layfolk's hands
the sacred text of the Gospel of Jesus Christ? Who
does not know instances, even in our own days, of
pious old women (especially in Ireland) chancing
to light upon a Bible (which they have never seen
before) and reading it (especially St. John's
Gospel 3:16) and going to the priest about the new
light they had received through the blessed
words, and then the priest snatching it out of

their hands and throwing it into the fire? This is not at all uncommon (it is said) in Catholic lands, where the poor people sometimes chance to get a copy of God's Word through the devoted labors of Bible-women and tract distributors. A Scotch lady in Rome, now happily a Catholic but then a member of a Protestant congregation there which supports a Bible distributor, once informed me of the account that this gentleman gravely related to a meeting of the congregation as to how an old woman in a small Italian town, accepting one of his Testaments and being illuminated by the Gospel of St. John (which she never saw before, of course, though part of it is read every day at Holy Mass), straightway went and confuted her priest and silenced him, so that he had no word to say in reply. This, I repeat, is the commonly accepted idea about Rome and her attitude toward Holy Scripture among the masses of non-Catholic people.

I have said advisedly "among the masses," for happily there are now a goodly number of enlightened and impartial persons and of scholars who have studied the matter fairly for themselves— men, for example, of the stamp of the late Dr. S. R. Maitland, among whom the idea is quite exploded. And one may not blame the masses too severely for entertaining the notion above alluded to: how indeed, we may ask, could they possibly think otherwise in face of the tradition handed down to them from their forefathers since the "Reformation" by minister, teacher and parents, through sermon, catechism, newspaper, books of travel, fiction and history? They have believed the tradition as naturally as they believed that the sun rose in the east and set in the west; or that monasteries and convents were sinks of iniquity and dens of corruption; or that there was once a female Pope called Joan; or that Catholics pay money to get their sins forgiven. You cannot blame them altogether, for they had, humanly speaking, no opportunity of knowing anything else.

The Protestant account of pre-Reformation Catholicism has been largely a falsification of history. All the faults and sins that could possibly be raked up or invented against Rome or against particular bishops or priests were presented to the people of this unhappy land, and all her best acts misconstrued, misjudged, misrepresented, and nothing of good told in her favor. She has been painted as all black and hideous, and no beauty could be seen in her. Consequently people came to believe the tradition as a matter of course, and accepted it as history, and no more dreamed of inquiring whether it was true or not than they dreamed of questioning whether Mary wrote the Casket Letters or blew up Darnley at Kirk o' Field. Add to this the further fact that, Catholicism being almost totally wiped out in Scotland, the people had no means of making themselves personally acquainted with either its doctrines or its practices, and being very imperfectly educated till the beginning of the nineteenth century, were as incapable of arriving at a true knowledge of the interior life of the Catholic Church as of the internal organism of an antediluvian tadpole. Hence one can easily understand how it came about that, among the mass of the people in Bible-loving Scotland, the Pope was recognized as the Anti-Christ foretold by St. John, and Rome herself, that sitteth upon the seven hills, identified as "Babylon, the Great, the mother of harlots, and abominations of the earth," and the "woman drunken with the blood of the saints."

The story goes that one day the Merry Monarch, Charles the Second, propounded to the learned and scientific men about the Court the following profound problem: How is it that a dead fish weighs less than a living one? The learned and scientific men discussed the grave difficulty and wrote elaborate treatises on it to please the Royal inquirer, but came to no satisfactory conclusion. Finally it occurred to one of them to test whether it really was as the King had said; and of course he discovered that the thing was a joke: the fish weighed exactly the same dead or living, and all the time the Merry Monarch had been "having them on." People have been acting much in the same way in regard to the assertion so glibly made that Rome hates the Bible, and persecutes it, and tries to blot it out of existence. But nowadays many are inquiring: Is it really so? Are we sure of our facts? Are we not building up mountains of abuse and calumny on a false supposition? Just as all have come to know that the sun, as a matter of fact, does not rise or set but stands still, that there never was a Pope Joan but his name was John, that monasteries and convents are homes of learning and sanctity and charity, and that no Catholic ever pays or ever could pay a single farthing to get his sins remitted—and all this through the spread of knowledge and education and enlightenment and study—so also I venture to think that people will now be rightly considered ignorant and blameworthy, and at the least behind the times, if they do not learn that the notion I have alluded to above about the Catholic Church and the Bible is false and nonsensical—historically false and inherently nonsensical. By a calm consideration of the facts of history and a mind open to conviction on genuine evidence, they will be driven by sheer force of honesty to the conclusion that the Catholic Church, so far from being the monster of iniquity that she is painted, has in very truth been the parent, the author and maker, under God, of the Bible; that she has guarded it and defended it all through the ages, and preserved it from error or destruction; that she has ever held it in highest veneration and esteem, and has grounded her doctrines upon it; that she alone has the right to call it her book; that she alone possesses the true Bible and the whole Bible, and that copies of the Scriptures existing outside of her pale are partly incorrect and partly defective, and that whatever in them is true, is true because derived from her who alone possesses the Book in its fullness and its truth. If they were Catholics, they would love God's Holy Word more and more; they would understand it better; they would adore the Divine Providence that took such a wise and sure means of preserving and perpetuating it; and they would profoundly admire the Catholic Church for her ceaseless vigilance, untiring zeal and unswerving fidelity to the commission entrusted to her by Almighty God.

∽ 1 ∽

Some Errors Removed

NOW, in order to understand properly the work of the Catholic Church in creating and defending and perpetuating the Holy Scriptures, we must say a few preliminary words as to the human means used in their production, and as to the collecting of the Books of the Bible as we have it at present. There are some common erroneous ideas which we would do well to clear away from our minds at the very outset.

1. To begin with, the Bible did not drop down from Heaven ready-made, as some seem to imagine; it did not suddenly appear upon the earth, carried down from Almighty God by the hand of angel or seraph; but it was written by men like ourselves, who held in their hand pen (or reed) and ink and parchment, and laboriously traced every letter in the original languages of the East. They were divinely inspired certainly, as no others ever have been before or since; nevertheless, they were human beings, men chosen by God for the work, making use of the human instruments that lay to their hand at the time.

2. In the second place we shall do well to remember that the Bible was not written all at once, or by one man, like most other books with

which we are acquainted, but that 1500 years elapsed between the writing of Genesis (the first Book of the Old Testament) and the Apocalypse or Revelation of St. John (the last Book of the New). It is made up of a collection of different books by different authors, forming, in short, a library instead of a single work, and hence called in Greek, "*Biblia*," or "the Books." If you had lived in the days immediately succeeding the death of Moses, all you would have had given to you to represent the Bible would have been the first five books of the Old Testament, written by that patriarch himself; that was the Bible in embryo, so to speak—the little seed that was to grow subsequently into a great tree, the first stone laid on which was gradually to be erected the beautiful temple of the written Word throughout the centuries that followed. From this we can see that the preacher extolling the Bible as the only comfort and guide of faithful souls was slightly out of his reckoning when he used these words: "Ah, my brethren! What was it that comforted and strengthened Joseph in his dark prison in Egypt? What was it that formed his daily support and meditation? What but that blessed book, the Bible!" As Joseph existed before a line of the Old Testament was penned, and about 1800 years before the first of the New Testament books saw the light, the worthy evangelist was guilty of what we call a slight anachronism.

3. Nor will it be out of place to remark here that the Bible was not written originally in Eng-

lish or Gaelic. Some folks speak as if they believed that the Sacred Books were first composed, and the incomparable Psalms of David set forth, in the sweet English tongue, and that they were afterwards rendered into barbarous language such as Latin or Greek or Hebrew for the sake of inquisitive scholars and critics. This is not correct; the original language, broadly speaking, of the Old Testament was Hebrew; that of the New Testament was Greek. Thus our Bibles as we have them today for reading are "translations"— that is, are a rendering or equivalent in English of the original Hebrew and Greek as it came from the pen of Prophet and Apostle and Evangelist. We see this plainly enough in the title page of the Protestant New Testament—which reads "New Testament of Our Lord and Saviour Jesus Christ, translated out of the original Greek."

4. A last point must always be kept clearly in mind, for it concerns one of the greatest delusions entertained by Protestants and makes their fierce attacks on Rome appear so silly and irrational— the point, namely, that the Bible, as we have it now, was not printed in any language at all till about 1500 years after the birth of Christ, for the simple reason that there was no such thing as printing known before that date. We have become so accustomed to the use of the printing press that we can scarcely conceive of the ages when the only books known to men were in handwriting; but it is the fact that, had we lived and flourished before Mr. John Gooseflesh discovered the

art of printing in the 15th century, we should have had to read our Testaments and our Gospels from the manuscript of monk or friar, from the pages of parchment or vellum or paper covered with the handwriting, sometimes very beautiful and ornamental, of the scribe that had undertaken the slow and laborious task of copying the Sacred Word. Protestants in these days send shiploads of printed Bibles abroad, and scatter thousands of Testaments hither and thither in every direction for the purpose of evangelizing the heathen and converting sinners, and declare that the Bible, and the Bible only, can save men's souls. What, then, came of those poor souls who lived before the Bible was printed, before it was even written in its present form? How were nations made familiar with the Christian religion and converted to Christianity before the 15th century? Our Divine Lord, I suppose, wished that the unnumbered millions of human creatures born before the year 1500 should believe what He had taught and save their souls and go to Heaven at least as much as those of the 16th and 20th centuries; but how could they do this when they had no Bibles, or were too poor to buy one, or could not read it even though they bought it, or could not understand it even if they could read it? On the Catholic plan (so to call it) of salvation through the teaching of the Church, souls may be saved and people become saints, and believe and do all that Jesus Christ meant them to believe and do—and, as a matter of fact, this has happened—in all

∽**2**∽

The Making of the
Old Testament

NOW, looking at the Bible as it stands today, we find it is composed of 73 separate books—46 in the Old Testament, and 27 in the New. How has it come to be composed precisely of these 73* and no others, and no more and no less? Well, taking first the Old Testament, we know that it has always been divided into three main portions—the Law, the Prophets and the Writings. (1) The Law, as I remarked before, was the nucleus, the earliest substantial part, which at one time formed the sole book of Scripture that the Jews possessed. Moses wrote it and placed a copy of it in the Ark; that was about 3300 years ago. (2) To this were added, long afterward, the Prophets and the Writings, forming the complete Old Testament. At what date precisely the volume or "canon" of the Old Testament was finally closed and recognized as completed forever is not absolutely certain.

---

*The number of books in the Catholic Bible is counted as 72 or 73 depending on whether *The Lamentations of Jeremias* is considered to be part of *Jeremias* or a separate book of the Old Testament. —*Publisher*, 2004.

When was the Old Testament compiled? Some would decide for about the year 430 B.C., under Esdras and Nehemias, resting upon the authority of the famous Jew, Josephus, who lived immediately after Our Lord and who declares that since the death of Ataxerxes, B.C. 424, "no one had dared to add anything to the Jewish Scriptures, to take anything from them, or to make any change in them." Other authorities, again, contend that it was not till near 100 B.C. that the Old Testament volume was finally closed by the inclusion of the "Writings." But whichever contention is correct, one thing at least is certain, that by this last date—that is, for 100 years before the birth of Our Blessed Lord—the Old Testament existed precisely as we have it now.

Of course, I have been speaking so far of the Old Testament, in Hebrew, because it was written by Jewish authority, in the Jewish language— namely, Hebrew—for Jews, God's chosen people. But after what is called the "Dispersion" of the Jews, when that people was scattered abroad and settled in many other lands outside Palestine, and began to lose their Hebrew tongue and gradually became familiar with "Greek, which was then a universal language, it was necessary to furnish them with a copy of their Sacred Scriptures in the Greek language. Hence arose that translation of the Hebrew Old Testament into Greek known as the *Septuagint*. This word means in Latin *70*, and is so named because it is supposed to have been the work of 70 translators, who performed their task at Alexandria, where there was a large Greek-speaking colony of Jews. Begun about 280 or 250 years before Christ, we may safely say that it was finished in the next century; it was the acknowledged Bible of all the "Jews of the Dispersion" in Asia, as well as in Egypt, and was the version used by Our Lord, His Apostles and Evangelists, and by Jews and Gentiles and Christians in the early days of Christianity. It is from this version that Jesus Christ and the New Testament writers and speakers quote when referring to the Old Testament.

But what about the Christians in other lands who could not understand Greek? When the Gospel had been spread abroad, and many people embraced Christianity through the labors of Apostles and missionaries in the first two centuries of our era, naturally they had to be supplied with copies of the Scriptures of the Old Testament (which was the inspired Word of God) in their own tongue; and this gave rise to translations of the Bible into Armenian and Syriac and Coptic and Arabic and Ethiopic for the benefit of the Christians in these lands. For the Christians in Africa, where Latin was best understood, there was a translation of the Bible made into Latin about 150 A.D., and, later, another and better for the Christians in Italy; but all these were finally superseded by the grand and most important version made by St Jerome in Latin called the "Vulgate"—that is, the common, or current or accepted version. This was in the fourth century of our era [A.D.]. By the time St. Jerome was born, there was great need of securing a correct and uniform text of Holy Scripture in Latin, for there was danger, through the variety and corrupt conditions of many translations then existing, lest the pure Scripture should be lost. So Jerome, who was a monk, and perhaps the most learned scholar of his day, at the command of Pope St. Damascus in 382 A. D. made a fresh Latin version of the New Testament (which was by this time practically settled), correcting the existing versions by the earliest Greek manuscripts (MSS.) he could find. Then in his cell at Bethlehem, between (approximately) the years 392-404, he also translated the Old Testament into Latin directly from the Hebrew (and not from the Greek Septuagint)—except the Psalter [book of Psalms], which he had previously revised from existing Latin versions. This Bible was the celebrated *Vulgate*, the official text in the Catholic Church, the value of which all scholars admit to be simply inestimable, and which continued to influence all other versions and to hold the chief place among Christians down to the Reformation. I say the "official" text, because the Council of Trent in 1546 issued a decree stamping it as the only recognized and authoritative version allowed to Catholics. "If anyone does not receive the entire books with all their parts as they are accustomed to be read in the Catholic Church, and in the old Latin Vulgate Edition, as sacred and canonical . . . let him be anathema." The Vulgate was revised under Pope Sixtus V in 1590, and again under Pope Clement VIII in 1593, who is responsible for the present standard text. It is from the Vulgate that our English Douay Version comes; and it is of this same Vulgate that the Commission under Cardinal Gasquet, by command of the Pope, is trying to find or restore the original text as it came from the hands of St. Jerome, uncorrupted by and stripped of subsequent admixtures with other Latin copies.*

---

*This work was begun in the pontificate of Pope St. Pius X (1903-1914) but was not completed and published until 1978. It is known as the *New Vulgate* or *Nova Vulgata* and was promulgated by Pope John Paul II as the *editio typica*. This edition of the Vulgate, however, does not give the hallmark Vulgate rendering of *Genesis* 3:15: "I will put enmities between thee and the woman, and thy seed and her seed: *she* shall crush thy head, and thou shalt lie in wait for *her* heel." (Emphasis added.) —*Publisher*, 2004.

❧ 3 ❧

The Church Precedes The New Testament

S O FAR, we have been dealing with rather dry material. We have seen how the Old Testament books came to be collected into one volume; now it remains to see how the Catholic Church also composed and selected and formed into another volume the separate books of the New Testament.

1. Now you will remember what I said before, that the New Testament was not, any more than the Old, all written at one time, or all by one man, but that at least 40 years passed away between the writing of the first and the writing of the last of its books. It is made up of the four Gospels, 14 Epistles of St. Paul, two of St. Peter, one of St. James, one of St. Jude, three of St. John, together with the Apocalypse of St. John, and the Acts of Apostles by St. Luke, who also wrote the third Gospel; so that we have, in this collection, works by at least eight different writers; and from the year that the earliest book was composed (probably the Gospel of St. Matthew) to the year that St. John composed his Gospel, about half a century had elapsed. Our Blessed Lord Himself never, so

far as we know, wrote a line of Scripture—certainly none that has been preserved. He never told His Apostles to write anything. He did not command them to commit to writing what He had delivered to them: but He said, "Go ye and teach all nations," "preach the Gospel to every creature," "He that heareth you heareth Me." What He commanded and meant them to do was precisely what He had done Himself, namely, deliver the Word of God to the people by the living voice— convince, persuade, instruct, convert them by addressing themselves face to face to living men and women; not entrust their message to a dead book which might perish and be destroyed, and be misunderstood and misinterpreted and corrupted, but adopt the more safe and natural way of presenting the truth to them by word of mouth, and of training others to do the same after they themselves were gone, and so, by a living tradition, preserving and handing down the Word of God as they had received it, to all generations.

2. And this was, as a matter of fact, the method the Apostles adopted. Only five out of the twelve wrote down anything at all that has been preserved to us; and of that, not a line was penned till at least 10 years after the death of Christ, for Jesus Christ was crucified in 33 A.D., and the first of the New Testament books was not written till about 45 A.D. You see what follows? The Church and the Faith existed before the Bible; that seems an elementary and simple fact which no one can deny or ever has denied. Thousands of people

became Christians through the work of the Apostles and missionaries of Christ in various lands, and believed the whole truth of God as we believe it now, and became Saints, before ever they saw or read, or could possibly see or read, a single sentence of inspired Scripture of the New Testament, for the simple reason that such Scripture did not then exist. How, then, did they become Christians? In the same way, of course, that pagans become Catholics nowadays, by hearing the truth of God from the lips of Christ's missionaries. When the twelve Apostles met together in Jerusalem and portioned out the known world among themselves for purposes of evangelization, allotting one country to one Apostle (such as India to St. Thomas), and another to another, how did they propose to evangelize these people? By presenting each one with a New Testament? Such a thing did not exist, and, we may safely say, was not even thought of. Why did Our Lord promise them the gift of the Holy Ghost and command them to be "witnesses" of Him? And why, in fact, did the Holy Ghost come down upon the Twelve and endow them with the power of speaking in various languages? Why but that they might be able to "preach the Gospel to every creature" in the tongue of every creature.

3. I have said that the Apostles at first never thought of writing the New Testament; and neither they did. The books of the New Testament were produced and called forth by special circumstances that arose, were written to meet particu-

lar demands and emergencies. Nothing was further from the minds of the Apostles and Evangelists than the idea of composing works which should be collected and formed into one volume and so constitute the Holy Book of the Christians. And we can imagine St. Paul staring in amazement if he had been told that his Epistles, and St. Peter's, and St. John's and the others would be tied up together and elevated into the position of a complete and exhaustive statement of the doctrines of Christianity, to be placed in each man's hand as an easy and infallible guide in faith and morals, independent of any living and teaching authority to interpret them. No one would have been more shocked at the idea of his letters usurping the place of the authoritative teacher, the Church, than the great Apostle who himself said, "How shall they hear without a preacher? How shall they preach unless they be sent? Faith cometh by hearing, and hearing by the Word of Christ." The fact is that no religion yet known has been effectually propagated among men except by word of mouth, and certainly everything in the natural and spiritual position of the Apostles on the one hand, and of the Jews on the other, was utterly unfavorable to the spread of Christianity by means of a written record.

The Jewish people were not used to it, and the Gentiles could not have understood it. Even Protestant authors of the highest standing are compelled to admit that the living teaching of the Church was necessarily the means chosen by

Jesus Christ for the spread of His Gospel, and
that the committing of it to writing was a later
and secondary development. Dr. Westcott, Bishop
of Durham, than whom among Anglicans there is
not a higher authority, and who is reckoned,
indeed, by all as a standard scholar on the Canon
of Scripture, says (*The Bible in the Church*—pp.
53 and following): "In order to appreciate the
Apostolic age in its essential character, it is necessary to dismiss not only the ideas which are
drawn from a collected New Testament, but those
also, in a great measure, which spring from the
several groups of writings of which it is composed.
The first work of the Apostles, and that out of
which all their other functions grew, was to
deliver in living words a personal testimony to
the cardinal facts of the Gospel—the Ministry, the
Death and the Resurrection of Our Lord. It was
only in the course of time, and under the influence
of external circumstances, that they committed
their testimony, or any part of it, to writing. Their
peculiar duty was to preach. That they did, in
fact, perform a mission for all ages in perpetuating the tidings which they delivered was due, not
to any conscious design which they formed, nor to
any definite command which they received, but to
that mysterious power . . . The repeated experience of many ages has even yet hardly sufficed to
show that a permanent record of His words and
deeds, open to all, must co-exist with the living
body of the Church, if that is to continue in pure
and healthy vigour." And again: "The Apostles,

when they speak, claim to speak with Divine authority, but they nowhere profess to give in writing a system of Christian Doctrine. Gospels and Epistles, with the exception, perhaps, of the writings of St. John, were called out by special circumstances. There is no trace of any designed connection between the separate books, except in the case of the Gospel of St. Luke and the Acts (also by St. Luke), still less of any outward unity or completeness in the entire collection. On the contrary, it is not unlikely that some Epistles of St. Paul have been lost, and though, in point of fact, the books which remain do combine to form a perfect whole, yet the completeness is due not to any conscious co-operation of their authors, but to the will of Him by whose power they wrote and wrought."

What a contrast there is, in these clear words of the great scholar, to the common delusion that seems to have seized some minds—that the Bible, complete and bound, dropped down among the Christians from Heaven after the day of Pentecost; or, at the least, that the Twelve Apostles sat down together in an upper room, pens in hand, and wrote off at a sitting all the Books of the New Testament! And allow me to give one more short quotation to drive home the point I am laboring at, that the written New Testament could never have been intended as the only means of preaching salvation. "It was some considerable time after Our Lord's Ascension" (writes the Protestant author of *Helps to the Study of the Bible*,

p. 2), "before any of the books contained in the New Testament were actually written. The first and most important work of the Apostles was to deliver a personal testimony to the chief facts of the Gospel history. Their teaching was at first *oral*, and it was no part of their intention to create a permanent literature." These, I consider, are valuable admissions.

4. But now, you may say, "What was the use of writing the Gospels and Epistles then at all? Did not God inspire men to write them? Are you not belittling and despising God's Word?" No, not at all; we are simply putting it in its proper place, the place that God meant it to have; and I would add, the Catholic Church is the only body in these days which teaches infallibly that the Bible, and the whole of it, *is* the Word of God, and defends its inspiration, and denounces and excommunicates anyone who would dare to impugn its Divine origin and authority.

I said before, and I repeat, that the separate books of the New Testament came into being to meet special demands, in response to particular needs, and were not, nor are they now, absolutely necessary either to the preaching or the perpetuating of the Gospel of Christ.

It is easy to see how the Gospels arose. So long as the Apostles were still living, the necessity for written records of the words and actions of Our Lord was not so pressing. But when the time came for their removal from this world, it was highly expedient that some correct, authoritative, reliable account be left of Our Lord's life by those who had known Him personally, or at least were in a position to have first-hand, uncorrupted information concerning it. And this was all the more necessary because there were being spread abroad incorrect, unfaithful, indeed altogether spurious Gospels, which were calculated to injure and ridicule the character and work of Our Divine Redeemer. St. Luke distinctly declares that this was what caused him to undertake the writing of his Gospel—"Forasmuch as *many have taken in hand* to set forth in order a narration of the things that have been accomplished among us." (*Luke* 1:1). He goes on to say that he has his information from eyewitnesses, and has come to know all particulars from the very beginning, and therefore considers it right to set them down in writing, to secure a correct and trustworthy account of Christ's life. So St. Matthew, St. Mark, St. Luke and St. John penned their Gospels for the use of the Church, the one supplying often what another omits, but yet none pretending to give an exhaustive or perfect account of all that Jesus Christ said and did, for if this had been attempted, St. John tells us, "the whole world would not have contained the books that would be written" about it. The Gospels, then, are incomplete and fragmentary, giving us certainly the most important things to know about Our Saviour's earthly life, but still not telling us all we might know, or much we do know in fact now and understand better, through the teaching of the

Catholic Church, which has preserved traditions handed down since the time of the Apostles, from one generation to another. These Gospels were read, as they are now among Catholics, at the gatherings of the Christians in the earliest days on the Sundays—not to set forth a scheme of doctrine that they knew already, but to animate their courage, to excite their love and devotion to Jesus Christ, and impel them to imitate the example of that Beloved Master whose sayings and doings were read aloud in their ears.

Well, now, what I said about the Gospels is equally true of the Epistles, which make up practically the whole of the rest of the New Testament. They were called into existence at various times to meet pressing needs and circumstances; were addressed to particular individuals and communities in various places, and not to the Catholic Church at large. The thought furthest from the mind of the writers was that they should ever be collected into one volume and made to do duty as a complete and all-sufficient statement of Christian faith and morals.

How did they arise? In this natural and simple way: St. Peter, St. Paul and the rest went forth to various lands, preaching the Gospel, and made thousands of converts, and in each place founded a church, and left priests in charge, and a bishop sometimes (as, *e.g.*, St. Timothy in Ephesus). Now these priests and converts had occasion many a time to consult their spiritual father and founder, like St. Paul, or St. Peter, or St. James, on many points of doctrine or discipline, or morals; for we must not imagine that at that date, when the Church was in its infancy, things were so clearly seen or understood or formulated as they are now. It was, of course, the same Faith then as always; but still there were many points on which the newly made Christians were glad to consult the Apostles, who had been sent out with the unction of Jesus Christ fresh upon them—points of dogma and ritual and government and conduct which they alone could settle. And so we find St. Paul writing to the Ephesians (his converts at Ephesus), or to the Corinthians (his converts at Corinth), or to the Philippians (his converts at Philippi), and so on to the rest (14 Epistles in all). And for what reason? Either in answer to communications sent to him from them, or because he had heard from other sources that there were some things that required correction in these places. All manner of topics are dealt with in these letters, sometimes in the most homely style. It might be to advise the converts, or to reprove them; to encourage them or instruct them; or to defend himself from false accusations. It might be, like that to Philemon, a letter about a private person as Onesimus, the slave.

But whatever the Epistles deal with, it is clear as the noonday sun that they were written just at particular times to meet particular cases that occurred naturally in the course of his missionary labors, and that neither St. Paul nor any of the other Apostles, intended by these letters to set

forth the whole theology or scheme of Christian
salvation any more than Pope Pius X intended to
do so in his Decree against the Modernists, or in
his Letter on the Sanctification of the Clergy. The
thing seems plain on the face of it. Leo XIII writes
to the Scotch Bishops on the Holy Scriptures, for
example; or Pius X to the Eucharistic Congress in
London on the Blessed Sacrament, or publishes a
Decree on Frequent Communion; or, again, one of
our Bishops, say, sends forth a letter condemning
secret societies, or issues a pastoral dealing with
the new marriage laws—are we to say that these
documents are intended to teach the whole way of
salvation to all men? That they profess to state
the whole Catholic creed? The question has only
to be asked to expose its absurdity. Yet precisely
the same question may be put about the position
of St. Paul's Epistles. True, he was an Apostle, and
consequently inspired, and his letters are the
written Word of God, and therefore are a final and
decisive authority on the various points of which
they treat, if properly understood; but that does
not alter the fact that they nowhere claim to state
the whole of Christian truth, or to be a complete
guide of salvation to anyone; they already pre-
suppose the knowledge of the Christian Faith
among those to whom they are addressed; they
are written to believers, not to unbelievers; in one
word, the Church existed and did its work before
they were written, and it would still have done so
even though they had never been written at all.
St. Paul's letters (for we are taking his merely as

a sample of all) date from the year 52 A.D. to 68 A.D.; Jesus Christ ascended to Heaven, leaving His Church to evangelize the world, 33 A.D.; and we may confidently assert that the very last place we should expect to find a complete summary of Christian doctrine is in the Epistles of the New Testament.

There is no need to delay further on the matter. I think I have made it clear enough how the various books of the New Testament took their origin. And in so explaining the state of the case, we are not undervaluing the written Word of God, or placing it on a level inferior to what it deserves. We are simply showing the position it was meant to occupy in the economy of the Christian Church. It was written by the Church, by members (Apostles and Evangelists) of the Church; it belongs to the Church, and it is her office, therefore, to declare what it means. It is intended for instruction, meditation, spiritual reading, encouragement, devotion, and also serves as proof and testimony of the Church's doctrines and Divine authority; but as a complete and exclusive guide to Heaven in the hands of every man—this it never was and never could be.

The Bible *in* the Church; the Church *before* the Bible—the Church the *Maker* and *Interpreter* of the Bible—that is right. The Bible above the Church; the Bible independent of the Church; the Bible, and the Bible only, the Religion of Christians—that is wrong. The one is the Catholic position; the other the Protestant.

∽4∽

Catholic Church Compiles
The New Testament

NOW we know that the Gospels and Epistles of the New Testament were read aloud to the congregations of Christians that met on the first day of the week for Holy Mass (just as they are still among ourselves): one Gospel here, another there; one Epistle of St. Paul in one place, another in another; all scattered about in various parts of the world where there were bodies of Christians. And the next question that naturally occurs to us is: When were these separate works gathered together so as to form a volume, and added to the Old Testament to make up what we now call the Bible?

Well, they were not collected for the best part of 300 years. So that here again, I am afraid, is a hard nut for Protestants to crack, namely, that though we admit that the separate works composing the New Testament were now in existence, yet they were for centuries not to be found altogether in one volume, were not obtainable by multitudes of Christians, and even were altogether unknown to many in different parts of the world. How, then, could they possibly form a guide to

Heaven and the chart of salvation for those who had never seen or read or known about them? It is a fact of history that the Council of Carthage, which was held in 397 A.D., mainly through the influence of St. Augustine, settled the Canon or Collection of New Testament Scriptures as we Catholics have them now and decreed that its decision should be sent on to Rome for confirmation. No Council (that is, no gathering of the Bishops of the Catholic Church for the settlement of some point of doctrine) was ever considered to be authoritative or binding unless it was approved and confirmed by the Roman Pontiff, while the decisions of every General Council that has received the approval of Rome are binding on the consciences of all Catholics. The Council of Carthage, then, is the first known to us in which we find a clear and undisputed catalogue of all the New Testament books as we have them in Bibles now.

It is true that many Fathers and Doctors and writers of the Church in the first three centuries from time to time mention by name many of the various Gospels and Epistles; and some, as we come nearer 397, even refer to a collection already existing in places. For example, we find Constantine, the first Christian Emperor, after the Council of Nicea, applying to Eusebius, Bishop of Cæsarea and a great scholar, to provide fifty copies of the Christian Scriptures for public use in the churches of Constantinople, his new capital. This was in 332 A.D. The contents of these copies are known to us: perhaps (according to some, even probably) one of these very copies of Eusebius' handiwork has come down to us; but they are not precisely the same as our New Testament, though very nearly so. Again, we find lists of the books of the New Testament drawn up by St. Athanasius, St. Jerome, St. Augustine and many other great authorities, as witnessing to what was generally acknowledged as inspired Scripture in their day and generation and country; but I repeat that none of these corresponds perfectly to the collection in the Bible that we possess now; we must wait till 397 for the Council of Carthage before we find the complete collection of New Testament books settled as we have it today, and as all Christendom had it till the sixteenth century, when the Reformers changed it.

You may ask me, however, what was the difference between the lists of New Testament books found in various countries and different authors before 397, and the catalogue drawn up at the Council of that date? Well, that introduces us to a very important point which tells us eloquently of the office that the Catholic Church performed, under God the Holy Ghost, in selecting and sifting and stamping with her Divine authority the Scriptures of the New Law; and I make bold to say that a calm consideration of the part that Rome took in the making and drawing up and preserving of the Christian Scriptures will convince any impartial mind that to the Catholic Church alone, so much maligned, we owe it that we know what the New Testament should consist of, and why precisely it consists of these books and of no others; and that without her we should, humanly speaking, have had no New Testament at all, or, if a New Testament, then one in which works spurious and works genuine would have been mixed up in ruinous and inextricable confusion.

I have used the words "spurious" and "genuine" in regard to the Gospels and Epistles in the Christian Church. You are horrified, and hold up your hands and exclaim: "Lord, save us! Here we have a Higher Critic and a Modernist." Not at all, Dear Reader; quite the reverse, I assure you. Observe, I have said "in the Christian Church"— I did not say "in the Bible," for there is nothing spurious in the Bible. But why? Simply because the Roman See in the fourth century of our era prevented anything spurious being admitted into it. There were spurious books floating about "in the Christian Church," without a doubt, in the early centuries; this is certain, because we know their very names; and it is precisely in her rejection of these, and in her guarding the collection of inspired writings from being mixed up with them, that we shall now see the great work that the Catholic Church did, under God's Holy Spirit, for all succeeding generations of Christians, whether within the fold or outside of it. It is through the Roman Catholic Church that Protestants have got their Bible; there is not (to paraphrase some words of Newman) a Protestant that vilifies and condemns the Catholic Church for her treatment of Holy Scripture but owes it to that Church that he has the Scripture at all. What Almighty God might have done if Rome had not handed down the Bible to us is a fruitless speculation with which we have nothing whatever to do. It is a contingent possibility belonging to an order of things which has never existed, except in imagination. What we are concerned with is the order of things and the sequence of history in which we are now living, and which we know, and which consequently God has divinely disposed; and in this providential arrangement of history it is a fact, as clear as any other historical fact, that Almighty God chose the Catholic Church, and her only, to give us His Holy Scriptures, and to give us them as we have them now, neither greater nor less. This I shall now proceed to prove.

(i) Before the collection of New Testament books was finally settled at the Council of Carthage, 397, we find that there were three distinct classes into which the Christian writings were divided. This we know (and every scholar admits it) from the works of early Christian writers like Eusebius, Jerome, Epiphanius and a whole host of others that we could name. These classes were (1) the books "acknowledged" as Canonical, (2) books "disputed" or "controverted," (3) books declared "spurious" or false.

Now in class (1), *i.e.*, those acknowledged by Christians everywhere to be genuine and authentic and to have been written by Apostolic men, we find such books as the Four Gospels, 13 Epistles of St. Paul, Acts of the Apostles. These were recognized east and west as "Canonical," genuinely the works of the Apostles and Evangelists whose names they bore, worthy of being in the "Canon" or sacred collection of inspired writings of the Church and read aloud at Holy Mass.

But there was (2) a class—and Protestants should particularly take notice of the fact, as it utterly undermines their Rule of Faith, "the Bible and the Bible only"—of books that were disputed, controverted: in some places acknowledged, in others rejected; and among these we actually find the Epistle of St. James, Epistle of St. Jude, 2nd Epistle of St. Peter; 2nd and 3rd of St. John, Epistle to the Hebrews and the Apocalypse of St. John. There were doubts about these works; perhaps, it was said, they were not really written by Apostles, or Apostolic men, or by the men whose names they carried. In some parts of the Christian world they were suspected, though in others unhesitatingly received as genuine. There is no getting out of this fact, then: Some of the books of our Bible which we, Catholic and Protestant alike, now recognize as inspired and as the written Word of God, were at one time, and indeed for long, viewed with suspicion, doubted, disputed, as not possessing the same authority as the others. (I am speaking only of the New Testament books; the same could be proved, if there were space, of the Old Testament; but the New Testament suffices abundantly for the argument.) But further still—what is even more striking and is equally fatal to the Protestant theory—in this (2) class of "controverted" and doubtful books, some were to be found which are not now in our New Testament at all, but which were by many then considered to be inspired and Apostolic, or were actually read at the public worship of the Christians, or were used for instructions to the newly-converted—in short, ranked in some places as equal to the works of St. James or St. Peter or St. Jude. Among these we may mention specially the "Shepherd" of Hermas, Epistle of Barnabas, the Doctrine of the Twelve Apostles [Didache], Apostolic Constitutions, Gospel according to the Hebrews, St. Paul's Epistle to the Laodiceans, Epistle of St. Clement, and others. Why are these not in our Bible today? We shall see in a minute.

Lastly, (3) there was a class of books floating about before 397 A.D. which were never acknowledged as of any value in the Church, nor treated as having Apostolic authority, seeing that they were obviously spurious and false, full of absurd fables, superstitions, puerilities, and stories and miracles of Our Lord and His Apostles which made them a laughingstock to the world. Of these some have survived and we have them today, to let us see what stamp of writing they were; most have perished. But we know the names of about 50 Gospels (such as the Gospel of James, the Gospel of Thomas, and the like), about 22 Acts (like the Acts of Pilate, Acts of Paul and Thecla, and others), and a smaller number of Epistles and

Apocalypses. These were condemned and rejected wholesale as "Apocrypha"—that is, false, spurious, uncanonical.

(ii) This then being the state of matters, you can see at once what perplexity arose for the poor Christians in days of persecution when they were required to surrender their sacred books. The Emperor Diocletian, for example, who inaugurated a terrible war against the Christians, issued an edict in 303 A.D. that all the churches should be razed to the ground and the Sacred Scriptures should be delivered up to the pagan authorities to be burned. Well, the question was: What was Sacred Scripture? If a Christian gave up an inspired writing to the pagans to save his life, he thereby became an apostate: he denied his Faith, he betrayed his Lord and God; he saved his life, indeed, but he lost his soul. Some did this and were called "traditores," traitors, betrayers, "deliverers up" (of the Scriptures). Most, however, preferred martyrdom, and refusing to surrender the inspired writings, suffered the death. But it was a most perplexing and harrowing question they had to decide—what really was Sacred Scripture? I am not bound to go to the stake for refusing to give up some "spurious" Gospel or Epistle. Could I, then, safely give up some of the "controverted" or disputed books, like the Epistle of St. James, or the Hebrews, or the Shepherd of Hermas, or the Epistle of St. Barnabas, or of St. Clement? There is no need to be a martyr by mistake. And so the stress of persecution had the effect of making still more urgent the necessity of deciding once and for all what was to form the New Testament. What, definitely and precisely, were to be the books for which a Christian would be bound to lay down his life on pain of losing his soul?

(iii) Here, as I said before, comes in the Council of Carthage, 397 A.D., confirming and approving the decrees of a previous Council (Hippo, 393 A.D.), declaring, for all time to come, what was the exact collection of sacred writings thenceforth to be reckoned, to the exclusion of all others, as the inspired Scripture of the New Testament. That collection is precisely that which Catholics possess at this day in their Douay Bible. That decree of Carthage was never changed. It was sent to Rome for confirmation. As I have already remarked, a Council, even though not a general Council of the whole Catholic Church, may yet have its decrees made binding on the whole Church by the approval and will of the Pope. A second Council of Carthage, over which St. Augustine presided in 419 A.D., renewed the decrees of the former one and declared that its act was to be notified to Boniface, Bishop of Rome, for the purpose of confirming it. From that date all doubt ceased as to what was and what was not "spurious," or "genuine," or "doubtful" among the Christian writings then known. Rome had spoken. A Council of the Roman Catholic Church had settled it. You might hear a voice here or there, in East or West, in subsequent times, raking up some old doubt, or raising a question as to whether this or that book of the New Testament is really what it claims to be or should be where it is. But it is a voice in the wilderness.

Rome had fixed the "Canon" of the New Testament. There are henceforward but two classes of books—inspired and not inspired. Within the covers of the New Testament all is inspired; all without, known or unknown, is uninspired. Under the guidance of the Holy Ghost the Council declared "This is genuine, that is false"; "this is Apostolic, that is not Apostolic." She sifted, weighed, discussed, selected, rejected, and finally decided what was what. Here she rejected a writing that was once very popular and reckoned by many as inspired and was actually read as Scripture at public service; there, again, she accepted another that was very much disputed and viewed with suspicion, and said: "This is to go into the New Testament." She had the evidence before her; she had Tradition to help her; and above all she had the assistance of the Holy Spirit, to enable her to come to a right conclusion on so momentous a matter. And in fact, her conclusion was received by all Christendom until the sixteenth century, when, as we shall see, men arose rebelling against her decision and altering the Sacred Volume. But, at all events in regard to the New Testament, the Reformers left the books as they found them, and today their Testament contains exactly the same books as ours; and what I wish to drive home is that they got these books from Rome, that without the Roman Catholic Church they would not

have gotten them, and that the decrees of
Carthage, 397 and 419 A.D., when all Christianity was Roman Catholic—reaffirmed by the Council of Florence, 1442, under Pope Eugenius IV, and
the Council of Trent, 1546—these decrees of the
Roman Church, and these only, are the means
and the channel and the authority which
Almighty God has used to hand down to us His
written Word. Who can deny it? The Church
existed before the Bible; she made the Bible; she
selected its books, and she preserved it. She
handed it down. Through her we know what is the
Word of God, and what the word of man; and
hence to try at this time of day, as many do, to
overthrow the Church by means of this very
Bible, and to put it above the Church, and to
revile her for destroying it and corrupting it—
what is this but to strike the mother that reared
them; to curse the hand that fed them; to turn
against their best friend and benefactor; and to
repay with ingratitude and slander the very guide
and protector who has led them to drink of the
water out of the Saviour's fountains?

❦5❧

Deficiencies of the Protestant Bible

(1) THE point that we have arrived at now, if you remember, is this: The Catholic Church, through her Popes and Councils, gathered together the separate books that Christians venerated which existed in different parts of the world; sifted the chaff from the wheat, the false from the genuine; decisively and finally formed a collection—*i.e.*, drew up a list or catalogue of inspired and apostolic writings into which no other book should ever be admitted, and declared that these and these only were the Sacred Scriptures of the New Testament. The authorities that were mainly responsible for thus settling and closing the "Canon" of Holy Scripture were the Councils of Hippo and of Carthage in the fourth century, under the influence of St. Augustine (at the latter of which two Legatees were present from the Pope), and the Popes Innocent I in 405, and Gelasius, 494, both of whom issued lists of Sacred Scripture identical with that fixed by the Councils. From that date all through the centuries this was the Christian's Bible. The Church never admitted any other; and at the

Council of Florence in the 15th century and the
Council of Trent in the 16th and the [First] Council of the Vatican in the 19th she renewed her
anathemas against all who should deny or dispute this collection of books as the inspired Word
of God.

(2) What follows from this is self-evident. The
same authority which made and collected and
preserved these books, alone has the right to
claim them as her own and to say what the meaning of them is. The Church of St. Paul and St.
Peter and St. James in the first century was the
same Church as that of the Council of Carthage
and of St. Augustine in the fourth, and of the
Council of Florence in the 15th, and of the Vatican
in the 19th—one and the same body—growing
and developing, certainly, as every living thing
must do, but still preserving its identity and
remaining essentially the same body, as a man of
80 is the same person as he was at 40, and the
same person at 40 as he was at 2. The Catholic
Church of today, then, may be compared to a man
who has grown from infancy to youth, and from
youth to middle age. Suppose a man wrote a letter setting forth certain statements; whom would
you naturally ask to tell what the meaning of
these statements was? Surely the man that wrote
it. The Church wrote the New Testament; she,
and she alone, can tell us what the meaning of it
is.

Again, the Catholic Church is like a person who
was present at the side of Our Blessed Lord when

He walked and talked in Galilee and Judea. Suppose, for a moment, that that man was gifted with perpetual youth (this, by the way, is an illustration from W. H. Mallock's, *Doctrine and Doctrinal Disruption*, chap. xi) and also with perfect memory, and had heard all the teaching and explanations of Our Redeemer and of His Apostles, and retained them; he would be an invaluable witness and authority to consult, surely, so as to discover exactly what was the doctrine of Jesus Christ and of the Twelve. But such undoubtedly is the Catholic Church: not an individual person, but a corporate personality who lived with, indeed was called into being by, Our Divine Saviour; in whose hearing He uttered all His teaching; who listened to the Apostles in their day and generation, repeating and expounding the Saviour's doctrine; who, ever young and ever strong, has persisted and lived all through the centuries, and continues even till our own day fresh and keen in memory as ever, and able to assure us, without fear of forgetting, or mixing things up, or adding things out of his own head, what exactly Our Blessed Lord said, and taught, and meant, and did.

Suppose, again, that the man we are imagining had written down much of what he heard Christ and the Apostles say, but had not fully reported all, and was able to supplement what was lacking by personal explanations which he gave from his perfect memory: that, again, is a figure of the Catholic Church. She wrote down much, indeed, and most important parts of Our Lord's teaching, and of the Apostolic explanation of it, in Scripture; but nevertheless she did not intend it to be a complete and exhaustive account, apart from her own explanation of it; and, as a matter of fact, she is able from her own perpetual memory to give fuller and clearer accounts, and to add some things that are either omitted from the written report, or are only hinted at, or partially recorded, or mentioned merely in passing.

Such is the Catholic Church in relation to her own book, the New Testament. It is hers because she wrote it by her first Apostles, and preserved it and guarded it all down the ages by her Popes and Bishops; nobody else has any right to it whatsoever, any more than a stranger has the right to come into your house and break open your desk and pilfer your private documents. Therefore, I say that for people to step in, 1500 years after the Catholic Church had had possession of the Bible, and to pretend that it is theirs, and that they alone know what the meaning of it is, and that the Scriptures alone, without the voice of the Catholic Church explaining them, are intended by God to be the guide and rule of faith—this is an absurd and groundless claim. Only those who are ignorant of the true history of the Sacred Scriptures—their origin and authorship and preservation—could pretend that there is any logic or common sense in such a mode of acting. And the absurdity is magnified when it is remembered that the Protestants did not appropriate the *whole* of the Catholic books, but actually cast out some from the collection, and took what remained, and elevated these into a new "Canon," or volume of Sacred Scripture, such as had never been seen or heard of before, from the first to the sixteenth century, in any Church, either in Heaven above or on earth beneath, or in the waters under the earth! Let us make good this charge.

(3) Open a Protestant Bible, and you will find there are seven complete Books wanting—that is, seven books fewer than there are in the Catholic Bible, and seven fewer than there were in every collection and catalogue of Holy Scripture from the fourth to the sixteenth century. Their names are Tobias, Baruch, Judith, Wisdom, Ecclesiasticus, I Machabees, II Machabees, together with seven chapters of the Book of Esther, and 66 verses of the 3rd chapter of Daniel, commonly called "The Song of the Three Children" (*Daniel* 3:24-90, Douay version). These were deliberately cut out, and the Bible bound up without them. The criticisms and remarks of Luther, Calvin and the Swiss and German Reformers about these seven books of the Old Testament show to what depths of impiety those unhappy men had allowed themselves to fall when they broke away from the true Church. Even in regard to the New Testament, it required all the powers of resistance on the part of the more conservative Reformers to prevent Luther from flinging out the Epistle of St. James as unworthy to remain within the volume of Holy Scripture—"an Epistle

of straw," he called it, "with no character of the Gospel in it." In the same way, and almost to the same degree, he dishonored the Epistle of St. Jude and the Epistle to the Hebrews and the beautiful Apocalypse of St. John, declaring they were not on the same footing as the rest of the books and did not contain the same amount of Gospel (*i.e., his* Gospel). The presumptuous way, indeed, in which Luther, among others, poured contempt and doubt upon some of the inspired writings which had been acknowledged and cherished and venerated for 1000 or 1200 years would be scarcely credible were it not that we have his very words in cold print, which cannot lie, and may be read in his biography or be seen quoted in such books as Dr. Westcott's *The Bible in the Church*. And why did he impugn such books as we have mentioned? Because they did not suit his new doctrines and opinions. He had arrived at the principle of private judgment—of picking and choosing religious doctrines; and whenever any book, such as the Book of Machabees, taught a doctrine that was repugnant to his individual taste—as, for example, that "it is a holy and wholesome thought to pray for the dead, that they may be loosed from sins" (*2 Mach.* 12:46)—well, so much the worse for the book; "Throw it overboard," was his sentence, and overboard it went. And it was the same with passages and texts in those books which Luther allowed to remain and pronounced to be worthy to find a place within the boards of the new Reformed Bible. In short, he not only cast out certain books, but he mutilated some that were left. For example, not pleased with St. Paul's doctrine, "We are justified by faith," and fearing lest good works (a Popish superstition) might creep in, he added the word "only" after St. Paul's words, making the sentence run: "We are justified by faith only," and so it reads in Lutheran Bibles to this day [1911]. An action such as that must surely be reprobated by all Bible Christians. What surprises us is the audacity of the man that could coolly change by a stroke of the pen a fundamental doctrine of the Apostle of God, St. Paul, who wrote, as all admitted, under the inspiration of the Holy Ghost. But this was the outcome of the Protestant standpoint, individual judgment: no authority outside of oneself. However ignorant, however stupid, however unlettered, you may—indeed, you are bound to—cut and carve out a Bible and a Religion for yourself. No Pope, no Council, no Church shall enlighten you or dictate or hand down the doctrines of Christ. And the result we have seen in the corruption of God's Holy Word.

(4) Yet, in spite of all reviling of the Roman Church, the Reformers were forced to accept from her those Sacred Scriptures which they retained in their collection. Whatever Bible they have today, disfigured as it is, was taken from us. Blind indeed must be the Evangelical Christian who cannot recognize in the old Catholic Bible the quarry from which he has hewn the Testament he loves and studies—but with what loss! At what a

6

The Originals and Their Disappearance

I. NOW, you may naturally enough ask me: "But how do you know all this? Where has the Bible come from? Have you got the original writings that came from the hand of Moses, or Paul, or John?" No, none of it, not a scrap or a letter, but we know from the Church's Tradition that these were the books they wrote, and they have been handed down to us in a most wonderful way. What we have now is the printed Bible; but before the invention of printing in 1450, the Bible existed only in handwriting—what we call manuscript—and we have in our possession now copies of the Bible in manuscript (MS.) which were made as early as the 4th century, and these copies, which you can see with your own eyes at this day, contain the books which the Catholic Bible contains today, and that is another way we know we are right in receiving these books as Scripture, as genuinely the work of the Apostles and Evangelists. Why is it that we have not the originals written by St. John and St. Paul and the rest? Well, there are several reasons to account for the disappearance of the originals.

49

(1) The persecutors of the Church for the first 300 years of Christianity destroyed everything Christian that they could lay their hands on. Over and over again, barbarous pagans burst in upon Christian cities, and villages and churches, and burned all the sacred things they could find. And not only so, but they especially compelled Christians (as we saw before) to deliver up their sacred books, under pain of death, and then consigned them to the flames. Among these, doubtless, some of the writings that came from the hand of the Apostle and Evangelist perished.

(2) Again, we must remember, the material which the inspired authors used for writing their Gospels and Epistles was very easily destroyed; it was perishable to a degree. It was called papyrus (I shall explain what it was made of in a moment), very frail and brittle, and not made to last to any great age; and its delicate quality, no doubt, accounts for the loss of some of the choicest treasures of ancient literature, as well as of the original handwriting of the New Testament writers. We know of no MS of the New Testament existing now which is written on papyrus.

(3) Furthermore, when in various churches throughout the first centuries copies were made of the inspired writings, there was not the same necessity for preserving the originals. The first Christians had no superstitious or idolatrous veneration for the Sacred Scriptures, such as seems to prevail among some people today; they did not consider it necessary for salvation that the very

handwriting of St. Paul or St. Matthew should be preserved, inspired by God though these men were; they had the living, infallible Church to teach and guide them by the mouth of her Popes and Bishops and to teach them not only all that could be found in the Sacred Scriptures, but the true meaning of it as well; so that we need not be surprised that they were content with mere *copies* of the original works of the inspired writers. As soon as a more beautiful or correct copy was made, an earlier and rougher one was simply allowed to perish. There is nothing strange or unusual in all this; it is just what holds good in the secular world. We do not doubt the terms or provisions of the Magna Charta because we have not seen the original; a copy, if we are sure it is correct, is good enough for us.

II. Well, then, the originals, as they came from the hand of Apostle and Evangelist, have totally disappeared. This is what infidels and skeptics taunt us with and cast in our teeth: "You cannot produce," they say, "the handwriting of those from whom you derive your religion, neither the Founder nor His Apostles; your Gospels and Epistles are a fraud; they were not written by these men at all, but are the invention of a later age; and consequently we cannot depend upon the contents of them or believe what they tell us about Jesus Christ." Now, of course, these attacks fall harmlessly upon us Catholics, because we do not profess to rest our religion upon the Bible alone, and are independent of it, and would be just as we are and what we are though there were no Bible at all. It is those who have staked their very existence upon that Book, and must stand or fall with it, that are called upon to defend themselves against the critics. But I shall only remark here that the argument of infidel and skeptic would, if logically applied, discredit not only the Bible, but many other books which they themselves accept and believe without hesitation. There is far more evidence for the Bible than there is for certain books of classical antiquity which no one dreams of disputing. There are, for example, only 15 manuscripts of the works of Herodotus, and none earlier than the 10th century A.D.; yet he lived 400 years before Christ. The oldest manuscript of the works of Thucydides is of the 11th century A.D.; yet he flourished and wrote more than 400 years before Christ. Shall we say, then, "I want to see the handwriting of Thucydides and Herodotus, else I shall not believe these are their genuine works. You have no copy of their writings near the time they lived; none, indeed, till 1400 years after them; they must be a fraud and a forgery"? Scholars with no religion at all would say we were fit for an asylum if we took up that position; yet it would be a far more reasonable attitude than that which they take up toward the Bible. Why? Because there are known to have been many thousand copies of the Testament in existence by the 3rd century—*i.e.*, only a century or two after St. John—and we know for certain there are 3000 existing at the present day, ranging from the fourth century downward. The fact is, the wealth of evidence for the genuineness of the New Testament is simply stupendous; and in comparison with many ancient histories which are received without question on the authority of late and few and bad copies, the Sacred Volume is founded on a rock. But let us pass on; it is enough for us to know that God has willed that the handiwork of every inspired writer, from Moses down to St. John, should have perished from among men, and that He has entrusted our salvation to something more stable and enduring than a dead book or an undecipherable manuscript—that is, the living and infallible Church of Christ: *Ubi Ecclesia, ibi Christus.* ["Where the Church is, there Christ is."]

Now I wish to devote what remains of this chapter to say something about the material instruments that were used for the writing and transmission of Holy Scriptures in the earliest days; and a brief review of the materials employed, and the dangers of loss and of corruption which necessarily accompanied the work, will convince us more than ever of the absolute need of some divinely protected authority like the Catholic Church to guard the Gospel from error and destruction, and preserve "the Apostolic deposit" (as it is called) from sharing the fate which is liable to overtake all things that are, as says St. Paul, contained in "earthen vessels."

III. Various materials were used in ancient times for writing, as, *e.g.*, stone, pottery, bark of trees, leather, and clay tablets among the Babylonians and Egyptians. (1) But before Christianity, and for the first few ages of our era, *Papyrus* was used, which has given its name to our "paper." It was formed of the bark of the reed or bulrush, which once grew plentifully on the Nile banks. First split into layers, it was then glued by overlapping the edges, and another layer glued to this at right angles to prevent splitting, and, after sizing and drying, it formed a suitable writing surface. Thousands of rolls of papyrus have been found in Egyptian and Babylonian tombs and beneath the buried city of Herculaneum, owing their preservation probably to the very fact of being buried, because, as I said, the substance was very brittle, frail and perishable, and unsuited for rough usage. Though probably many copies of the Bible were originally written on this papyrus (and most likely the inspired writers used it themselves), none have survived the wreck of ages. It is this material St. John is referring to when he says to his correspondent in his second Epistle, verse 12; "Having more things to write to you, I would not by paper and ink." (2) When in the course of time, papyrus fell into comparative disuse from its unsuitableness and fragility, the skins of animals came to be used. This material had two names; if it was made out of the skin of sheep or goats, it was called *Parchment*; if made of the skin of delicate young calves, it was called *Vellum*. Vellum was used in earlier days, but being very dear and hard to obtain, gave place to a large extent to the coarser parchment.

St. Paul speaks about this stuff when he tells St. Timothy to "bring the books, but especially the parchments." (2 Tim. 4:13). Most of the New Testament manuscripts which we possess today are written on this material. A curious consequence of the costliness of this substance was this, that the same sheet of vellum was made to do duty twice over, and became what is termed a *palimpsest*, which means "rubbed again." A scribe, say, of the tenth century, unable to purchase a new supply of vellum, would take a sheet containing, perhaps, a writing of the second century, which had become worn out through age and difficult to decipher; he would wash or scrape out the old ink, and use the surface over again for copying out some other work in which the living generation felt more interest. It goes without saying that in many cases the writing thus blotted out was of far greater value than that which replaced it; indeed, some of the most precious monuments of sacred learning are of this description, and they were discovered in this way. The process of erasing or sponging out the ancient ink was seldom so perfectly done as to prevent all traces of it still remaining, and some strokes of the older hand might often be seen peeping out beneath the more modern writing. In 1834 some chemical mixture was discovered which was applied with much success and had the effect of restoring the faded lines and letters of those venerable records. Cardinal Mai, a man of colossal scholarship and untiring industry, and a member of the Sacred College in

Rome under Pope Gregory XVI, was a perfect expert in this branch of research, and by his ceaseless labors and ferret-like hunts in the Vatican library brought to light some remarkable old manuscripts and some priceless works of antiquity. Among these, all students have to thank him for restoring a long lost work of Cicero (*De Republica*) that was known to have existed previously and which the Cardinal unearthed from beneath St. Augustine's *Commentary on the Psalms*! The most important MS. of the New Testament of this description is called the *Codex of Ephraem*. About 200 years ago it was noticed that this curious-looking vellum, all soiled and stained, and hitherto thought to contain only the theological discourses of St. Ephraem, an old Syrian Father, was showing dim traces and faint lines of some older writing beneath. The chemical mixture was applied, and lo, what should appear but a most ancient and valuable copy of Holy Scriptures of handwriting not later than the fifth century! This had been coolly scrubbed out by some impecunious scribe of the twelfth century to make room for his favorite work, the discourses of St. Ephraem! Let us charitably hope that the good monk (as he probably was) did not know what he was scrubbing out. At all events, it was brought into France by Queen Catherine de Medici and is now safely preserved in the Royal Library at Paris, containing on the same page two works, one written on top of the other with a period of 700 years between them.

I have told you about the sheets used by the earliest writers of the New Testament. What kind of pen and ink had they?

(1) Well, for the brittle papyrus, a reed was used, much the same as that still in use in the East; but of course for writing on hard, tough parchment or vellum a metal pen, or stylus, was required. It is to this St. John refers in his third Epistle (verse 12) when he says, "Having more things to write unto you, I would not by paper and ink." The strokes of these pens may still be seen quite clearly impressed on the parchment, even though all trace of the ink has utterly vanished. Besides this, a bodkin or needle was employed, by means of which, along with a ruler, a blank leaf or sheet was carefully divided into columns and lines; and on nearly all the manuscripts these lines and marks may still be seen, sometimes so firmly and deeply drawn that those on one side of the leaf have penetrated through to the other side, without, however, cutting the vellum.

(2) The ink used was a composition of soot or lampblack or burnt shavings of ivory, mixed with gum or winelees or alum (for all these elements entered into it). In most ancient manuscripts, unfortunately, the ink has for the most part turned red or brown, or become very pale, or peeled off or eaten through the vellum, and in many cases later hands have ruthlessly retraced the ancient letters, making the original writing look much coarser. But we know that many colored inks were used, such as red, green, blue or

purple, and they are often quite brilliant to this day.

(3) As to the shape of the MSS., the oldest form was that of a roll. They were generally fixed on two rollers, so that the part read (for example, in public worship) could be wound out of sight and a new portion brought to view. This was the kind of thing that was handed to Our Lord when He went into the synagogue at Nazareth on the Sabbath. "He unfolded the book", and read: and then "when he had folded the book, he restored it to the minister." (*Luke* 4:17, 20.) When not in use, these rolls were kept in round boxes or cylinders, and sometimes in cases of silver or cloth of great value. The leaves of parchment were sometimes of considerable size, such as folio; but generally the shape was what we know as quarto [about $9\frac{1}{2}$ x $12\frac{1}{2}$ inches] or small folio, and some were octavo. The skin of one animal, especially if an antelope, could furnish many sheets of parchment; but if the animal was a small calf, then its skin could only furnish very few sheets; and an instance of this is the manuscript called the *Sinaitic* (now in St. Petersburg), whose sheets are so large that the skin of a single animal (believed to have been the youngest and finest antelope) could only provide two sheets (8 pages).

(4) The page was divided into two or three or four columns (though the latter is very rare). The writing was of two distinct kinds, one called uncial (meaning an inch), consisting entirely of capital letters, with no connection between the

letters, and no space between words at all; the other style, which is later, was cursive (that is, a running hand) like our ordinary handwriting, with capitals only at the beginning of sentences; and in this case the letters are joined together and there is a space between words. The uncial style (consisting of capitals only) was prevalent for the first three centuries of our era; in the fourth century the cursive began and continued till the invention of printing.

(5) Originally, I need hardly say, there was no such thing in the MSS. as divisions into chapters and verses, and no points or full stops [i.e., periods] or commas, to let you know where one sentence began and the next finished: hence the reading of one of these ancient records is a matter of some difficulty to the unscholarly. The division into chapters so familiar to us in our modern Bibles was the invention either of Cardinal Hugo, a Dominican, in 1248, or more probably of Stephen Langton, Archbishop of Canterbury (d. 1227); and it is no calumny upon the reputation of either of these great men to say that the division is not very satisfactory. He is not fortunate in his method of splitting up the page of Scripture; the chapters are of very unequal length and frequently interrupt a narrative or argument or an incident in an inconvenient way, as anyone may see for himself by looking up such passages as Acts 21:40; or Acts 4 and 5, or 1 Corinthians 12 and 13. The division again into verses was the work of one Robert Stephens, and the first Eng-

lish version in which it appeared was the Geneva Bible, 1560. This gentleman seems to have completed his performance on a journey between Paris and Lyons (*inter equitandum*, as the Latin biographer phrases it), probably while stopping overnights in inns and hostels. "I think," an old commentator quaintly remarks, "it had been better done on his knees in the closet." To this I would venture to add that his achievement must share the same criticism of inappropriateness as the arrangement into chapters.

(6) The manuscripts of the Bible, as I before remarked, now known to be in existence, number about 3000, of which the vast majority are in running hand, and hence are subsequent to the fourth century. There are none of course later than the sixteenth century, for then the book began to be printed; and none have yet been found earlier than the fourth. Their age, that is, the precise century in which they were written, it is not always easy to determine. About the tenth century the scribes who copied them began to notify the date in a corner of the page; but before that time we can only judge by various characteristics that appear in the MSS. For example, the more simple and upright and regular the letters are, the less flourish and ornamentation they have about them, the nearer equality there is between the height and breadth of the characters—the more ancient we may be sure is the MS. Then, of course, we can often tell the age of a MS.—approximately, at least—by the kind of pictures

the scribe had painted in it, the illustrations he had introduced, and the ornamenting of the first letter of a sentence or on the top of a page; for we know in what century that particular style of illumination prevailed. It would be impossible to give anyone who had never seen any specimens of these wonderful old manuscripts a proper idea of their appearance or make him realize their unique beauty. There they are today, perfect marvels of human skill and workmanship, manuscripts of every kind: old parchments all stained and worn; books of faded purple lettered with silver, and their pages beautifully designed and ornamented; bundles of finest vellum, yellow with age, and bright even yet with the gold and vermilion laid on by pious hands 1000 years ago—in many shapes, in many colors, in many languages. There they are, scattered throughout the libraries and museums of Europe, challenging the admiration of everyone that beholds them for the astonishing beauty, clearness and regularity of their lettering, and the incomparable illumination of their capitals and headings—still at this day, after so many centuries of change and chance, charming the eye of all with their soft yet brilliant colors and defying our modern scribes to produce anything the least approaching them in loveliness. There lie the sacred records, hoary with age, fragile, slender, time-worn, bearing upon their front clear proofs of their ancient birth; yet with the bloom of youth still clinging about them. We simply stand and wonder; and we also despair. We

∽7∽

Variations in the Text
Fatal to Protestant Theory

I HAVE mentioned monasteries, and justly so, for there is no doubt that the vast majority, indeed practically all, of these venerable pages were traced by the hand of some ecclesiastic. The clergy were the only persons who had learning enough for it. What care, what zeal, what loving labor was spent by these holy men in their work of transcribing the word of Scripture, we can judge by viewing their handiwork. Yet the work was necessarily very slow and liable to error; and that errors did creep in we know from the simple fact that there are about 200,000 variations in the text of the Bible as written in these MSS. that we have today. This is not to be wondered at, if you remember that there are 35,000 verses in the Bible.

Consider the various ways in which corruptions and variations could be introduced. The variations might have been (a) intentionally introduced or (b) unintentionally. (a) Under this class we must unfortunately reckon those changes which were made by heretics to suit their particular doctrine or practice, just as, for example, the Lutherans added the word "only" to St. Paul's words to fit in with their new-fangled notion about "justification by faith only." Or again, a scribe might really think that he was improving the old copy from which he was transcribing by putting in a word here or leaving out a word there, or putting in a different word, so as to make the sentence clearer or the sense better. But (b) it is satisfactory to be assured (as we are) that the vast majority of changes and varieties of readings in these old MSS. is entirely due to some unintentional cause. (i) The scribe might be tired or sleepy or exhausted with much writing, and might easily skip over a word, or indeed a whole sentence; or miss a line or repeat a line; or make a mistake when he came to the end of a line or a sentence; he might be interrupted in his work and begin at the wrong word when he recommenced. Or he might (ii) have bad eyesight (some lost it altogether through copying so much); or not know really what was the proper division to make of the words he was copying, especially if the copy he was busy with was one of the old Uncials, with no stops and no pauses and no division between words or sentences; or he might, if he were writing at the dictation of another, not hear very well, or pick up a word or phrase wrongly, as, for example, the woman did when she wrote "Satan died here" for a milliner's shop, instead of "Satin dyed here." Or (iii) he might actually embody and copy into the sacred text of the Gospels words or notes or phrases which did not really belong to the

Gospel at all, but had been written on the margin of the parchment by some previous scribe merely to explain things. These "glosses," as they are called, undoubtedly have crept in to some copies, and the Protestants are guilty of repeating one every time they say their form of the Lord's Prayer, with its ending "For thine is the kingdom and the power and the glory forever. Amen." Such an addition was not uttered by Our Lord; Catholics consequently do not use it.

These are some (and not all) of the ways in which you could easily see that differences could arise in the various copies made by old scribes. Put six men today to report a speech by any orator; there will be considerable variety in their reports, as one can prove by comparing different newspaper accounts of the same speech any morning. I do not say that the differences will always signify much or substantially alter the speaker's meaning; yet there they are, and sometimes they may be serious enough; and if these things happen daily, even now with all our advanced and highly developed methods of printing, how much more would they happen in the old days before printing, when hand and brain and eyesight and hearing could make so many blunders? One single letter changed would conceivably reverse the meaning of the whole sentence. I shall not alarm you by flaunting specimens from the Greek or Hebrew, but shall make plain enough what I mean by recording an instance occurring in our own days in our own tongue. An old Provost of a certain East Lothian town had died and been duly buried, and a headstone had been erected bearing the fitting inscription from St. Paul's 1st Epistle to the Corinthians (15:52): "And we shall be changed." It was finished on the Saturday; but a deed of darkness was done before the "Sabbath" morning. The minister had a son who loved a practical joke. He got accomplices for his shameful deed; they hoisted him up, and in cold blood he took putty and obliterated the letter "c" in "changed." On the "Sabbath" the godly, passing around with long faces, Bibles and white handkerchiefs to view the old Provost's tombstone, learned for the first time that the Apostle taught: "And we shall be hanged."

You see what I mean? Well, the Bibles, before printing, are full of varieties and differences and blunders. Which of them all is correct? Pious Protestants may hold up their hands in horror and cry out, "there are no mistakes in the Bible! It is all inspired! It is God's own Book!" Quite true, *if you get God's own book*, the originals as they came from the hand of Apostle, Prophet and Evangelist. These, and these men only, were inspired and protected from making mistakes: but God never promised that every individual scribe (perhaps sleepy-headed, or stupid, or heretical) who took in hand the copying out of the New Testament would be infallibly secure from committing errors in his work. The original Scripture is free from error, because it has God for its author; so teaches the Catholic Church; and the

Catholic Bible, too, the Vulgate, is a correct version of the Scripture; but that does not alter the fact that there are scores, nay thousands, of differences in the old manuscripts and copies of the Bible that were written before the days of printing; and I should like any inquiring Protestants to ponder over this fact and see how they can possibly reconcile it with their principle that the Bible alone is the all-sufficient guide to salvation.

Which Bible? Are you sure you have got the right Bible? Are you certain that your Bible contains exactly the words, and all the words and only the words, that came from the hands of Apostle and Evangelist? Are you sure that no other words have crept in or that none have been dropped out? Can you study the Hebrew and Greek and Latin manuscripts and versions, page by page, and compare them, and compile for yourself a copy of Holy Scripture identical with that written by the inspired authors from Moses to St. John? If you cannot—and you see at once that it is impossible—then do not talk about "the Bible and the Bible only." You know perfectly well that you *must* trust to some authority outside of yourself to give you the Bible. The Bible you are using today was handed down to you: you have, in fact, allowed some third party to come between you and God, a thing quite repugnant to the Protestant theory. We Catholics, on the other hand, glory in having some third party to come between us and God, because God Himself has given it to us, namely, the Catholic Church, to teach us and lead us to Him. We believe in the Bible interpreted for us by that Church, because God entrusted to her the Bible as part of His word, and gave her a promise that she would never err in telling us what it means and explaining to us the "many things hard to be understood," which St. Peter tells us are to be found within it. Though there were as many million variations as there are thousands in the different copies of the Bible, we should be still unmoved, for we have a "Teacher sent from God," above and independent of all Scripture, who, assisted by the Holy Ghost, speaks with Divine authority, and whose voice to us is the Voice of God.

It matters not to us when a Christian may have lived on earth: whether before any of the New Testament was written at all, or before it was collected into one volume, or before it was printed, or after it has been printed; no matter to us whether there are 1,000 or 1,000,000 variations in texts and passages and chapters of ancient copies of which our modern Bibles are compiled; we do not hazard our salvation on such a precarious and unreliable support. We rather take that Guide who is "yesterday and today and the same for ever," and who speaks to us with a living voice, and who can never make a mistake; who is never uncertain or doubtful or wavering in her utterances, never denying today what she affirmed yesterday, but ever clear, definite, dogmatic; enlightening what is dark and making plain what is obscure to the minds of men. This is the

Catholic Church, established by Almighty God as His organ and mouthpiece and interpreter, unaffected by the changes and unshaken by the discoveries of ages. To her we listen; her we obey; to her we submit our judgment and our intellect, knowing she will never lead us wrong. In her we find peace and comfort, satisfaction and solution of all our difficulties, for she is the one infallible Teacher and Guide appointed by God. This is a logical, consistent, clear and intelligible method of attaining and preserving the truth, a perfect plan and scheme of Christianity. It is the Catholic plan; it is Christ's plan. What plan have any others to substitute for it that can stand a moment's analysis at the bar of reason, history, common sense, or even of Holy Scripture itself?

∾8∾

Our Debt to the Monks

THUS far we have been speaking of the Bible
as found written in the old manuscripts,
mostly in the very early centuries of
Christianity. Now the next question after settling
how the Bible was made and collected and committed to writing is: How was it preserved and
multiplied and diffused throughout the centuries
previous to the invention of printing? For you will
bear in mind that we are as yet a long way off the
day when the first printing press was invented or
set up. Did the people at large know anything at
all about the Sacred Scriptures before it was
printed and put into their hands? Here we are
suddenly plunged into the Middle Ages; what was
the history of the Holy Book during that time
which people in these countries generally call
"Dark"? If you have patience with me for a little I
shall prove to you that, just as the Catholic
Church at the very beginning wrote and collected
together the sacred books of the New Testament,
so by her monks and friars and clergy generally
she preserved them from destruction during the
Middle Ages and made the people familiar with
them; and, in short, that it is to the Roman
Church again, under God, that we owe the pos-

session of the Bible in its integrity at the present day.

Now of course, this will sound strange and startling in the ears of those who have imbibed the common notions about the Middle Ages. As I said there was a traditional Protestant delusion about the Catholic Church and the Bible in general, so there is a traditional opinion which every good Protestant must adopt about those Ages of Faith, as we Catholics prefer to call them. The general idea is that they were centuries (from the eighth century to the end of the fourteenth) of profound ignorance, oppression, superstition and of universal misery—that the monks were debauched, greedy and lazy—that the people in consequence were illiterate and immoral, only half civilized, and always fighting—that the whole of Europe was sunk in barbarism and darkness, men's intellects enslaved and their wills enervated, and all their natural energies paralyzed and benumbed by the blighting yoke of Rome—that (in the comprehensive language of the Church of England Homilies) "laity and clergy, learned and unlearned, all ages, sects and degrees of men, women and children, of whole Christendom, had been altogether drowned in damnable idolatry, and that by the space of 800 years and more." That is fairly sweeping. How they can reconcile that alleged state of things with the unconditioned promises of Our Blessed Lord that "the gates of hell should never prevail against the Church" and that He would "be with her always, to the end of the world," and that the "Holy Ghost would lead them into all the truth"—is to me a mystery. But let that pass. We are asked, then, to believe that during the Middle Ages true Christianity was overlaid and buried beneath a mass of Popish fables and traditions, and that of course the Bible in consequence was unknown except to a very few; was neglected and ignored and kept out of sight, because it would have destroyed Popery if it had been known. Only when the light of the Reformation shone out did the Holy Book appear openly in the world and become familiar to the faithful of Christ as that which was to "make them wise unto salvation."

Now, I am not going to enter into a general defense of the condition of things in the Catholic world during these Ages of Faith, though, if time permitted, nothing would be more congenial to me. I would merely remark in passing, however, that perhaps men of the 21st or 22nd century will take the very same view of this age of ours as some people do now of the Middle Ages, and will look back with horror upon it as a time when the world was desolated by famine, pestilence and war—when nations of the earth amassed huge armies and built immense navies to slaughter each other and plunder each other's territories—when the condition of the poor was harsher and crueller than ever before in the history of the world since Christ was born—when there were on the one side some hundreds or thousands of capitalists, with some millionaires among them; and on the other, many millions of the laboring classes in deepest want and misery; multitudes on the very verge of starvation, wondering how they were to keep a roof over their heads or get a bit of food for themselves and for their children. People in ages to come will, mayhap, regard this century with its boasted progress and civilization, and this land with 350 years of Protestantism behind it as an age and a country where drunkenness and dishonesty and immorality and matrimonial unfaithfulness and extravagance and unbelief and youthful excesses and insubordination and barbarity of manners were so universally and so deeply rooted that the authorities of the kingdom were simply helpless to cope with them. I am one of those who hold that the "Dark Ages" were ages full of light in comparison to these in which we are now living. The ages which built the gorgeous Cathedrals and Abbeys whose ruins still stand as silent but eloquent witnesses of their past glory and beauty, and still delight the eye and captivate the admiration of even the most unsympathetic beholder—those ages could at least not have been sunk in ignorance of architecture, or been insensible to the beautiful and the artistic, or been niggardly or ungenerous in their estimate of what was a worthy temple for the majesty of the God of Heaven and earth and a dwelling place fitting for the Lord of Hosts.

Again, the ages which covered the face of Europe with universities and schools of learning, which produced philosophers and theologians like St. Thomas Aquinas and St. Bonaventure, and Albertus Magnus and Scotus and Bacon, and which built up the scholastic system—a system which, for logical acuteness and metaphysical accuracy, for subtilty and unity and complete consistency, has never been equalled, and which still stands unshaken by all attacks and triumphing over all its rivals that "have their day and cease to be"—that age, I say, could hardly have been intellectually dark or barren. Once more: An age which produced saints like Dominic and Francis and Bernard and was fruitful in bringing forth Orders of men and women for assisting our poor humanity in every form and stage of its existence—teaching the ignorant, caring for the sick and the afflicted, and even redeeming captives from the yoke of slavery—the age, besides, which witnessed the Crusades, those magnificent outbursts of Christian chivalry and of loyalty to Jesus Christ Our Lord—when men, kings and princes and subjects, seizing the Crusader's cross, went cheerfully to lay down their lives in myriads on the burning plains of Syria in their glorious attempts to rescue the Holy Sepulchre from the hand of Turk and infidel—that age, I say, cannot have been altogether devoid of the love of Him who Himself gave His life for men, and Whose feet had trod those sacred places in the days of His Flesh. People speak glibly nowadays of the ignorance of these far back times; but it seems to me that no man who is really grounded in the truth of Christianity, who knows his *Pater Noster*, *Ave*, Creed, the Ten Commandments and the Seven Sacraments and puts them into practice, can ever be said to be truly ignorant. He might not have been able to build a motor car or even to drive one—to turn out a steamship or a flying machine or speak the weird language of Esperanto. Neither could St. Peter or St. Joseph, for that matter. Nevertheless, the practical teaching the people of those ages received from priest and monk in church and school was, I submit, of far more real moral and intellectual value than the hash of scraps of hygiene and science, French and cookery, civics and art which is crammed into the unwilling brain of our 20th-century public school children. Generally speaking, the medievalists, so despised, had the knowledge of God and of the world to come, and that was really the best knowledge they could have. (See preface to Dr. Maitland's *Dark Ages*.)

But I am afraid I have been guilty of a serious digression; what we must do now is to confine ourselves to the single point as to how the Scriptures were preserved and multiplied and made known to the people in the Middle Ages. (1) I shall first prove that the Bible was multiplied and preserved by the monks and priests. All must now admit that it was really in monasteries that multitudes of copies of the Holy Scriptures were made. Monasteries were centers of learning in those times even more than they are today, because education was not so widely spread. An indispensable part of the outfit of every monastery was a library. "A monastery without a library," writes a monk of the twelfth century to another monk, "is like a castle without an armory." And he goes on to declare that the great defense in the monastic armory should be the Bible. Sometimes the libraries were very large, and we read of Emperors and other great people borrowing from them. The monks were the most learned men of those days, and were by profession scholars, men who had renounced worldly pursuits and pleasures and dedicated themselves to a retired life of prayer and study; and one of the principal parts of their scholastic activity was the copying and transcribing of the Sacred Scriptures. For this purpose there was a large room called the Scriptorium in which a dozen or more monks could be engaged at one time, but there were also many monks employed each in his own cell, which contained all the necessary apparatus for literary work. These cells were so arranged around the central heating chamber that in winter their hands would not get benumbed with so much writing. Day by day, year after year, the monks would persevere in their holy labors, copy-

---

*A rough idea of the equivalent in today's U.S. dollar may be obtained by figuring that the British pound (£) was worth about $5.00 in 1911, when this book was first published. Moreover, the purchasing power of the American dollar (and of currencies in general) is today about 1/100th of what it was in 1911. Therefore, £70 in 1911 England would be equivalent to $35,000 in 2004. The sum of £218 in 1911 England would equal about $109,000 today. —*Publisher*, 2004.

ing with loving care every letter of the sacred text from some old manuscript of the Bible, adorning and illuminating the pages of vellum with pictures and illustrations in purple and gold and silver coloring, and so producing real works of art that excite the envy and admiration of modern generations. Some Bishops and Abbots wrote out with their own hands the whole of both the Old and the New Testaments for the use of their churches and monasteries. Even nuns—and this point I would bring under special notice—nuns took their share in this pious and highly skilled labor. We read of one who copied with her own hands two whole Bibles, and besides made six copies of several large portions of the Gospels and Epistles. Every monastery and church possessed at least one, and some possessed many copies of the Bible and the Gospels. In those ages it was a common thing to copy out particular parts of the Bible (as well as the whole Bible)—for example, the Gospels, or the Psalms, or Epistles, so that many who could not afford to purchase a complete Bible were able to possess themselves of at least some part which was specially interesting or popular. This custom is truly Catholic, as it flourishes among us today. At the end of our prayer books, for instance, we have Gospels and Epistles for the Sundays; and various publishers, too, have issued the four Gospels separately, each by itself, and the practice seems to me to harmonize entirely with the very idea and structure of the Bible, which was originally composed of separate and independent portions, in use in different Churches throughout Christendom. And so we find that the monks and clergy often confined their work to copying out certain special portions of Sacred Scripture, and naturally the Gospels were the favorite part.

The work, we must remember, was very slow, and expensive as well. Dr. Maitland reckons that it would require ten months for a scribe of those days to copy out a Bible, and that £60 or £70* would have been required if he had been paid at the rate that law stationers pay their writers. Of course, with the monks it was a labor of love, and not for money; but this calculation of Dr. Maitland only refers to the work of copying; it leaves out of account the materials that had to be used, pen and ink and parchment. Another authority (Buckingham) has made a more detailed calculation, and assuming that 427 skins of parchment would have been needed for the 35,000 verses, running into 127,000 folios, he reckons that a complete copy of Old and New Testaments could not have been purchased for less than £218.* Yet Protestants stare in astonishment when you tell them that not everybody could sit by his fireside in those days with a Bible on his knees! Some princes (among them, I think, Charlemagne) gave the monks permission to hunt for deer in the Royal forests so as to get skins to make into parchment for copying work.

I have no space to give elaborate proof of my assertion that, as a matter of course, all monasteries and churches possessed copies of the Scriptures in the Middle Ages. It stands to reason that those who made the copies would keep at least one for their own use in the monastery, and another for the public services in the church. We read of one convent in Italy which had not money enough for the bare necessaries of life, yet managed to scrape up £50 to purchase a Bible. Dr. Maitland, in his most valuable book *The Dark Ages*—he was a Protestant, librarian to the Archbishop of Canterbury, a great student, and a most impartial scholar—gives page after page of instances, that came under his own notice in his researches, of religious houses that had Bibles and Testaments in their possession. Of course these are but casual specimens; the thing was so common that there was no need to chronicle the fact any more than you would chronicle the fact that A or B had a clock in his parlor in the nineteenth century. Kings and Princes and Popes often presented beautiful copies of the Bible to Abbots and Priors for use in their monastery, sometimes gloriously embellished within with painting and illuminations, written in letters of gold and silver, and bound in golden casing set with gems. We frequently read of such gifts. And not only the Bible, but other books used in the service of the Church, such as copies of the Missal or Psalter or Gospels, all containing great portions of Holy Scripture, were often presented as gifts by great personages in Church or State, bound in gold or ivory or silver of the utmost purity, and marvelously adorned and studded with pearls and precious stones. Nothing was considered too costly or too magnificent to lavish on the Sacred Volume. But I suppose that when we find Popes like Leo III and Leo IV, and Emperors like Henry II and Lewis the Debonnaire, and Bishops like Hincmar of Rheims, and Dukes like Hugh of Burgundy, and Bishops like Ralph of Rochester, and numberless Abbots and Priors in the eighth and ninth centuries causing copies of the Sacred Scriptures to be made and gifted to monasteries and churches throughout Europe, this must be taken as evidence of Rome's hatred of the Word of God and her fear of its becoming known or read or studied! Yet that this was the common custom for hundreds of years is a fact of history that is quite beyond the region of doubt. Moreover, the Sacred Scriptures were a favorite subject of study among the clergy; and a popular occupation was the writing of commentaries upon them, as all priests at least are aware, from having to recite portions of them every day ranging from the age of St. Leo the Great and St. Gregory down to St. Bernard and St. Anselm.

(2) Now one could go on at any length accumulating evidence as to the fact of monks and priests reproducing and transmitting copies of the Bible from century to century, before the days of Wycliff and Luther; but there is no need, because I am not writing a treatise on the subject, but merely adducing a few proofs of my assertions and trying to show how utterly absurd is the contention that

Rome hates the Bible and did her best to keep it a locked and sealed book and even to destroy it throughout the Middle Ages. Surely nothing but the crassest ignorance or the blindest prejudice could support a theory so flatly contradicted by the simplest facts of history. The real truth of the matter is that it is the Middle Ages which have been a closed and sealed book to Protestants, and that only now, owing to the honest and patient researches of impartial scholars among them, are the treasures of those grand centuries being unlocked and brought to their view. It is this ignorance or prejudice which explains to me a feature that would be otherwise unaccountable in the histories of the Bible written by non-Catholics. I have consulted many of them, and they all, with hardly an exception, either skip over this period of the Bible's existence altogether or dismiss it with a few off-hand references. They jump right over from the inspired writers themselves, or perhaps from the fourth century, when the Canon was fixed, to John Wycliff, "The Morning Star of the Reformation," leaving blank the intermediate centuries, plunged, as they imagine, in worse than Egyptian darkness.

But I ask—Is this fair or honest? Is it consistent with a love of truth thus to suppress the fact, which is now happily beginning to dawn on the more enlightened minds, that it was the monks and clergy of the Catholic Church who, during all these ages, preserved, multiplied and perpetuated the Sacred Scriptures? The Bible on its human

heart not only the whole Psalter [Book of Psalms], but (as under the rule of St. Pachomius) the New Testament as well. I suppose most ministers of the Kirk [national church of Scotland] could stand this test quite easily.

Then the clergy were continually meditating on various portions of the Scriptures, and writing about them in homilies and commentaries, and ever reciting them in their services, so they could not help but know them well. Some of the Saints of those days, like St. Anselm and St. Hubert, actually knew them by heart, and could answer every question, however difficult, about the meaning of them. And not only Saints, but multitudes of ordinary priests and Bishops constantly had the Scriptures on their lips. Wulstan, Bishop of Worcester, for example, had a custom, which would be decidedly trying to most clergy in our days, of repeating the whole Psalter along with his attendant priests when journeying; and we are told that "lying, standing, walking, sitting, he had always a Psalm on his lips, always Christ in his heart." Again, we know of Abbots (like him of Cologne) who "caused the whole of the Old and the New Testaments to be read through every year." Besides, the Scriptures were read daily during meals in monasteries. And if further proof were required that the clergy were intimately familiar, not only with the words, but with the meaning and teaching of Holy Scripture, we have only to dip into the sermons, happily preserved, which these men preached to their flocks, and we shall find them simply full to overflowing with quotations from every part of the Bible—far fuller, indeed, than the sermons of Protestant clergy in the twentieth century. I shall give only one example, and we have no reason to think that it is at all exceptional.

It is the sermon of a monk called Bardo in Germany, who was about to be appointed Archbishop of Mentz. He preached, however, first before a great multitude at Christmas about the year 1000, the Emperor being present. His text was Psalm 17:13. I have not seen the whole of his sermon, but only about eight printed pages of it. I have counted the references and quotations from the Old and New Testaments, and I find there are exactly 73. The audience enjoyed the sermon, understood the references, and the monk was made Archbishop.

I hope I have shown now how really preposterous is the idea that the monks did not know the Bible. What man in his senses can have patience to listen to the silly legend that Martin Luther first discovered by accident the Scriptures—a book which, as a friar, he was bound to have known and studied and learned and recited for years? The simple fact, as is now proved by irrefutable evidence, is that the clergy of those "dark ages" had a knowledge of and familiarity with the written Word of God which modern ministers cannot equal; and what is no less important, together with their knowledge they had a deep veneration and love for it, guarding it jealously from corruption and error, believing what they taught, humbly accepting its Divine authorship and authority—an attitude in striking contrast to present day critics, who treat the Bible like a common book and pick holes in it and impugn its genuineness and its accuracy, and in general attempt to eliminate the supernatural element from it altogether.

(2) But, again, I think I hear the voice of the objector, who will not believe all this if he can possibly help it—"Yes; well, perhaps the clergy did know the Bible, but *nobody else did*; it was a closed and sealed volume to the poor lay people, because, of course, it was all in *Latin*." Now, leaving aside the question of Latin for a moment (for I shall come back to that immediately), it is utterly false to say or suppose that the lay folks were ignorant of the Scriptures. They were thoroughly well-acquainted with them so far as they required to be in their state of life. It is true, of course—and how could it be otherwise?—that ecclesiastics being the reading men and writing men—in short, the only well-educated persons of those days—naturally have left behind them more evidence than most lay people could do of their familiarity with the Sacred Word; but it is yet the fact that the literature of those ages, outside clerical documents altogether, which has come down to us, is steeped and permeated through and through with Scripture. Conversations, for example, correspondence, law deeds, household books, legal documents, historical nar-

ratives—all are full of it; full not only of the ideas, but often of the very words of Scripture. How many lawyers and doctors and professors and ordinary lay folks nowadays, I wonder, would be found quoting from the Bible in their writings? The reason, of course, was that books were scarce in those days, and expensive, and the Bible was the most common and popular and accessible; it was the most familiar to kings and princes, to soldiers and lawyers, to business men and tradesmen, laborers and artisans. They all knew it and understood it, and enjoyed the numberless quotations and references to it in sermons and addresses, and could often repeat portions of it from memory. "The writings of the dark ages"— says Dr. Maitland in chapter 27 of his most valuable and entertaining book, *The Dark Ages*—"the writings of the dark ages are, if I may use the expression, made of the Scriptures. I do not merely mean that the writers constantly quoted the Scriptures, and appealed to them as authorities on all occasions, as other writers have done since their day; but I mean that they thought and spoke and wrote the thoughts and words and phrases of the Bible, and that they did this constantly and habitually as the natural mode of expressing themselves. They did it, too, not exclusively in theological or ecclesiastical matters, but in histories, biographies, familiar letters, legal instruments, and documents of every description. I do not know that I can fully express my meaning, but perhaps I may render it more clear if I repeat that I do not so much refer to direct quotations of Scripture as to the fact that their ideas seem to have fallen so naturally into the words of Scripture that they were constantly referring to them in a way of passing allusion which is now very puzzling to those who are unacquainted with the phraseology of the Vulgate." We can thus see from the testimony of such a student of that period as Rev. Dr. Maitland how the language and ideas of the Bible had passed into the current language of the people. Sometimes persons carried copies of the Gospels about with them, just as Catholics today carry about them a Gospel of St. John, out of veneration.

(3) But how, it may be asked, could the people who were unable to read (and they were admittedly a large number) become acquainted with the Bible? The answer is simple. They were taught by monk and priest, both in church and school, through sermon and instruction. They were taught by sacred plays or dramas, which represented visibly to them the principal facts of sacred history, like the Passion Play of today at Oberammergau. They were taught through paintings and statuary and frescoes in the churches, which portrayed before their eyes the doctrines of the Faith and the truths of Scripture: and hence it is that in Catholic countries the walls of churches and monasteries and convents, and even cemeteries, are covered with pictures representing Scriptural scenes.

"Painting is the book of the ignorant." Stained

glass windows may be mentioned in the same category; and so may popular hymns, and poetry, and simple devotional books for the poor—all of which, along with the ceremonies and functions of the Church, served to imprint on people's memories and understandings the great events in God's dealings with His creatures since the beginning of the world. We must remember, too, that, for those who could not afford to purchase a Bible or a copy of the Gospels, the Sacred Volume was often chained to a stone in some public place about the church for everyone to study; and wealthy persons in their wills were known to leave money enough to provide for such a thing. The simple truth is that the Catholic Church adopted every means at her disposal in these old days to bring a knowledge of God's Word to those who could not read, as well as to those who could.

Bibles were not printed because there was no printing press; but whose fault was that? Is the Church to blame for not inventing printing sooner? But why did God not invent printing Himself if He wished the Bible to be in everybody's hand? Nero had no motor car, nor had Julius Caesar a maxim gun, nor William Wallace a flying machine—were these men consequently ignorant and behind the times and worthy of contempt? There were no railway trains in Luther's day; nor did John Knox invent chloroform, or Oliver Cromwell electricity—are these men in consequence to be considered as illiterate, stupid, barbarous, sunk in mental degradation? The

Catholic Church, then, had to do the best she could in the circumstances; and I submit she did all that any organization on earth could possibly have done for the spread of Scripture knowledge among her children. Vast numbers could not read, I admit it; the Church was not to blame for that. Latin was the universal tongue, and you had to be rather scholarly to read it. But I protest against the outrageous notion that a man cannot know the Bible unless he can read it. Can he not *see* it represented before his eyes? Can he not *hear* it read? Do you not know and understand one of Shakespeare's plays much better by *seeing* it acted on the stage than by reading it out of a book? Do the visitors to Oberammergau, witnessing the "Passion Play," not come to understand and realize the story of the Passion and Death of Our Lord more vividly by *seeing* it enacted before their eyes than if they read the cold print of a New Testament? You hear a Board School child rattling off the ten plagues of Egypt and the names of all the Kings of Israel and Juda, and divers chapters of the Bible: but does that child necessarily *know* what it is reciting? Does it understand and appreciate and realize? It may or it may not; there is no necessary connection between the two things.

There is such a thing as literal idolatry, worshipping the letter and neglecting the spirit: a superstitious, grovelling subserviency to the mere text of the Bible. A boy or girl might know whole passages of the Bible by heart, and only use them for their own moral ruin. I am contending for the genuine, real, practical working knowledge of the Bible among the generality of Catholics in the Middle Ages: and, whether they could read or not, I do not hesitate to assert that, with few exceptions, they had a personal and intelligent knowledge and a vivid realization of the most necessary facts in the Sacred Scripture and in the life of Our Divine Lord to an extent which is simply not to be found among the millions of our nominal Christians in these islands today. Whatever ignorance there was, this at least all impartial scholars must concede: the Church was in no way to blame for it. Where, I ask, is the proof of the Church's hatred of the Bible, of any attempt to hide it, to destroy it, to dishonor and belittle it? I cannot do better than give you here two or three sentences from the work of the learned and honest Protestant student, some of whose words I have quoted before: "I must add that I have not found anything about the arts and engines of hostility, the blind hatred of half-barbarian kings, the fanatical fury of their subjects, or the reckless antipathy of the Popes (in regard to the Bible). I do not recollect any instance in which it is recorded that the Scriptures, or any part of them, were treated with indignity, or with less than profound respect. I know of no case in which they were intentionally defaced or destroyed (except, as I have just stated, for their rich covers), though I have met with, and hope to produce several instances, in some of which they were the only, and in others almost

∽10∽

Where Then Are All
The Medieval Bibles?

BUT let us return for a moment to the popular objection (hinted at above): "Still, the Bible was in Latin; you cannot deny that. The Church kept it in Latin so the people should not read it. She was afraid of putting it into the common language of the people." There is some truth in these statements; but there is more untruth. That the Scriptures were for the most part in Latin is true; that it was because of the Church's dread of her people getting to know the Bible and so abandoning their Catholic faith is, of course, false.

(1) Bible in Latin. Admitting for the moment that the Bible was in Latin during the Middle Ages, what follows? That nobody but priests could read it? Nonsense. There were just two classes of people then: those who could read, and those who could not read. Now, those who did read could read Latin, and, therefore, were perfectly content with the Scriptures in Latin. Those who could not read Latin could not read at all. I ask, therefore, what earthly need was there of a translation of the Bible from Latin into the

language of the common multitude? What good would it have done? At this point we may expect to hear our friend indignantly giving vent to some such objection as this: "The people, then, were horribly illiterate; they could not write their own names; they could not read; they were half barbarian and savage; they were really fearfully ignorant, you know, and degraded. Just compare them for one moment with our present day School Board children in the matter of reading and writing and general intelligence."

Softly now, I answer; one thing at a time. We are not discussing that at present, and do not mean to discuss it, because it is beside the question. The Church was not to blame for the people's ignorance of letters; but let that pass—or even grant, if you like, for the sake of argument, that the Church was blameworthy; the point I am insisting on is only this—granted a man cannot read, what on earth is the use of putting a Bible in his hand in any language under Heaven, whether Greek or Hebrew, or Latin, or English, or Arabic? That man, if he is taught the Bible at all, must be taught it in other ways and by other means, as we have seen he was in the "Dark Ages." So that we arrive at this point: that either the Latin Bible was read, or no Bible at all. The learned Protestant author, Dr. Cutts , in his book, *Turning Points of English Church History*, refers to this fact when he says: "Another common error is that the clergy were unwilling that the laity should read the Bible for themselves, and carefully kept it in an unknown tongue, that the people might not be able to read it. The truth is that most people who could read at all could read Latin, and would certainly prefer to read the authorized Vulgate to any vernacular version"— *i.e.*, preferred the Latin Bible to an English one. Dr. Peter Bayne also deals with this point when he remarked in the *Literary World* (October, 1894), quoted by "M.C.L." in her booklet: "Latin was then the language of all men of culture, and, to an extent probably far beyond what we at present realize, the common language of Europe; in those days tens of thousands of lads, many of them poor, studied at the Universities, and learned to talk Latin." I may add that I came across the statement lately in the life of St. Peter Martyr, who flourished in the 13th century, that he gave some retreat or addresses to nuns in that age in Latin, and was understood by them.

The whole mistake in people's minds arises, of course, from the supposition they make that Latin was then a dead language, whereas it was really a living one in every sense of the term, being read and spoken and written universally in Europe, and consequently being understood by everyone who could read at all. What motive or purpose, then, could the Church have had in translating it into another tongue? In any case, this much none can help admitting—that at least the Church turned the Scriptures from Hebrew and Greek (which were the original languages) into Latin, which was the living language of the world, for the benefit of her children. She might still have kept the Bible a dark, unknown, mysterious document by leaving it in Hebrew and Greek. She did the very opposite. Does this seem as if she was anxious to keep her people in ignorance?

(2) However, we are not done with objections yet. "How is it," ask our Protestant friends, "that if, as you say, the Sacred Scriptures were multiplied and reproduced and copied over and over again hundreds and thousands of times, even in Latin, how is it that we have so few of these copies now? Where have they gone? Surely we should expect to have many of them preserved." The question, I am afraid, betrays an ignorance (not altogether inexcusable) of the condition of society and civilization and of international relations in these distant centuries. There were many causes at work which perfectly account for the disappearance of the majority of the old copies of the Bible. (*a*) To begin with, there was frequent, if not continual, war going on, during which books and manuscripts were ruthlessly destroyed. We need only mention such instances as the invasions of the Danes and Normans, and of the Saracens and northern barbarians into Italy, burning monasteries and churches, sacking and laying waste ecclesiastical buildings. During these oft-repeated incursions and the horrible pillage that generally accompanied warfare, many most valuable libraries and thousands of MSS. and copies of the Scriptures of rare, indeed

of priceless worth, must have perished. (*b*) Then there is the common occurrence of fire, which accounts for the loss of much valuable literature—by which copies of Scripture were burned, either by accident or by design, either singly or in the general conflagration that consumed the whole monastery or library as well. (*c*) Another very common cause of loss was negligence, through which, both in the Middle Ages and since, many invaluable books and papers have gone to destruction. Sometimes a book was borrowed from the conventual library and never returned. This became so great an evil that proprietors of books adopted the plan of inscribing an excommunication or a curse against those who should keep or steal what had been merely lent—much in the style of the anathemas pronounced in the Decrees of the Church's Councils.

For example, we find one case like this: "This book belongs to St. Mary of Robert's Bridge; whosoever shall steal it or sell it, or alienate it from this house, or mutilate it, let him be anathema maranatha, Amen." The librarian was not often as careful as he should have been over his treasures; so his books and MSS. were sometimes allowed to go amissing, or to be taken away, or to perish through damp, or corruption, or rats or mice, or water, or by being stolen, or even by being sold by those who had no right to sell, and to those who had no right to buy. Lastly, we know that great quantities of most important parchments and manuscripts have been used by bookbinders for such ignoble purposes as to form backs and bands and fly-leaves and covers of other books. (*d*) But over and above these simple and natural causes, there was another which we must not forget, and which was perhaps more far-reaching and powerful than the rest—I mean the deliberate destruction of the books and manuscripts so as to get the gold and silver and precious stones in which they were set and bound. I have spoken before of the costliness of the cases and ornaments that surrounded the copies of the Scriptures. Sometimes twenty pounds of pure gold were used in their binding, not to speak of the jewels that adorned their covers. Now, that rapacious and unscrupulous men, whether Catholic or Protestant, should in their lust for money seize upon these treasures, which were in the keeping of harmless and defenseless monks and priests, we can well understand; and that they did so is unfortunately only too true. Thousands of monasteries and libraries were rifled, an incalculable amount of ancient and precious books and parchments burned or otherwise destroyed, and their gold and silver settings turned into hard cash. For the Word of God they cared nothing; what they wanted was money. And if this were true, as it is to a limited extent, of Catholic days, what shall we say of the robberies and plunders committed by sectaries in England, in their first fury, at the Reformation? We can scarcely conceive the extent to which the Reformers went in their rage and hatred against everything that had the least semblance of Rome about it, especially if it seemed likely to afford them some "filthy lucre." The Protestant historian, Collier, tells how Henry VIII determined to "purge his library" of all Popish and superstitious books and consequently gave orders for the destruction of such things as "missals, legends, and suchlike"; but notice the next point of command—"to deliver the garniture of the books, being either silver or gold, to his officers." That was the real motive; avarice, cupidity, greed of gold. The books thus plundered and stripped of their precious stones were largely Bibles and copies of the Gospels. Fuller says: "The Holy Scriptures themselves, much as the Gospellers pretended to regard them, underwent the fate of the rest. If a book had a cross on it, it was condemned for Popery, and those with lines and figures were interpreted [as involving] the black art, and destroyed for conjuring." "Whole libraries," exclaims another, "were destroyed or made waste paper of, or consumed for the vilest uses . . . broken windows were patched with remnants of the most valuable MSS. on vellum, and the bakers consumed vast quantities in heating their ovens."

Collier, who is quoted above (he was an Anglican Bishop), writes: "One among the misfortunes consequent upon the suppression of monasteries was an ignorant destruction of a great many books. The books, instead of being removed to royal libraries, to those of Cathedrals, or the universities, were frequently thrown into grantees as things of small consideration. Now, these men

oftentimes proved a very ill protection for learning and for antiquity; their avarice was oftentimes so mean and their ignorance so
undistinguishing that, when the covers were
somewhat rich and would yield a little, they
pulled them off, and threw away the books or
turned them to wastepaper; and thus many noble
libraries were destroyed, to a great public scandal
and an irreparable loss to learning." That
Henry VIII caused the monasteries and convents
to be dissolved, and their books and treasures
plundered and pillaged wholesale in order to
replenish his coffers that were sorely depleted is
matter of history, though the ostensible reason
was, of course, zeal for the true religion and the
purifying of the morals of people and priests. How
far a sixteenth-century Nero like Henry VIII was
fitted to undertake such a work is a matter of
opinion. But certain it is that, in the diabolical
fury which the authorities of that day waged
against all Catholic institutions and monuments,
loads of priceless copies of the Sacred Scriptures
perished as utterly as though they had been
destroyed by the pagan persecutors of the first
four centuries after Christ. Listen (if you are not
tired of hearing of such atrocities) to the account
given by Dom Bede Camm, O.S.B., in his charming *Life of Cardinal Allen* (page 11), of the outrageous vandalism and hideous barbarities
perpetrated at Oxford in those fearful days. After
telling how the Chapel of All Souls was wrecked,
its images and altars defaced and desecrated, the

organs burned in the quadrangle and even the sacred pyx, in which the Body of the Lord had lain so long, cut down and broken into pieces, he goes on: "Terrible, too, to all who loved learning was the wanton destruction of priceless manuscripts. Cartloads of books were carried off to the fire or sold to merchants to wrap their wares in. Anything which these miserable men did not understand was condemned as savoring of superstition. All MSS. that were guilty of the superstition of displaying red letters on their fronts or tiles were doomed. Ribald young men carried great spoils of books on biers up and down the city, singing as at a mock funeral, and their priceless burdens were finally burned in the common marketplace. The story of it all as told by contemporaries is all but incredible. The University library was stripped so bare that even the very shelves were sold for firewood, and the quadrangles of New College were for days littered with torn manuscripts." I do not think I need say more on the point. It must be tolerably clear now where we should look for an answer to the question: "Where are all the old copies of the Bible that Catholics say the monks so lovingly and laboriously made in the Middle Ages?" The answer must be plainly found in the insensate greed and fanatical destructiveness on the part of the sixteenth-century Revolutionaries. Which side showed the more veneration and regard for God's written Word may be safely left to the judgment of all reflecting minds.

Abundance of Vernacular Scriptures before Wycliff

I HAVE said that people who could read at all in the Middle Ages could read Latin: hence there was little need for the Church to issue the Scriptures in any other language. But as a matter of fact, she did in many countries put the Scriptures in the hands of her children in their own tongue.

(1) We know from history that there were popular translations of the Bible and Gospels in Spanish, Italian, Danish, French, Norwegian, Polish, Bohemian and Hungarian for the Catholics of those lands before the days of printing, but we shall confine ourselves to England, so as to refute once more the common fallacy that John Wycliff was the first to place an English translation of the Scriptures in the hands of the English people in 1382.

To anyone that has investigated the real facts of the case, this fondly cherished notion must seem truly ridiculous; it is not only absolutely false, but stupidly so, inasmuch as it admits of such easy disproof; one wonders that nowadays any lecturer or writer should have the temerity to advance it. Now, observe I am speaking of the days before the printing press was invented; I am speaking of England, and concerning a Church which did not, and does not, admit the necessity of Bible-reading for salvation—and concerning an age when the production of the Scriptures was a most costly business, and far beyond the means of nearly everybody. Yet we may safely assert, and we can prove, that there were actually in existence among the people many copies of the Scriptures in the English tongue of that day. To begin far back, we have a copy of the work of Caedmon, a monk of Whitby, at the end of the seventh century, consisting of great portions of the Bible in the common tongue. In the next century we have the well-known translations of Venerable Bede, a monk of Jarrow, who died "while busy with the Gospel of St. John. In the same (eighth) century we have the copies of Eadhelm, Bishop of Sherborne; of Guthlac, a hermit near Peterborough; and of Egbert, Bishop of Holy Island; these were all in Saxon, the language understood and spoken by the Christians of that time. Coming down a little later, we have the free translations of King Alfred the Great who was working on the Psalms when he died, and of Aelfric, Archbishop of Canterbury; as well as popular renderings of Holy Scripture like the Book of Durham and the Rushworth Gloss and others that have survived the wreck of ages. After the Norman conquest in 1066, Anglo-Norman or Middle-English became the language of England, and consequently the next translations of the Bible we meet with are in that tongue. There are several specimens still known, such as the paraphrase of Orm (about 1150) and the *Salus Animae* (1250), the translations of William Shoreham and Richard Rolle, hermit of Hampole (died 1349). I say advisedly "specimens," for those that have come down to us are merely indications of a much greater number that once existed, but afterward perished. We have proof of this in the words of Blessed [now Saint] Thomas More, Lord Chancellor of England under Henry VIII, who says: "The whole Bible long before Wycliff's day was by virtuous and well-learned men translated into the English tongue, and by good and godly people with devotion and soberness well and reverently read." (*Dialogues*, III). Again: "The clergy keep no Bibles from the laity but such translations as be either not yet approved for good, or such as be already reproved for naught (*i.e.*, bad, naughty), as Wycliff's was. For, as for old ones that were before Wycliff's days, they remain lawful and be in some folks' hand. I myself have seen, and can show you, Bibles, fair and old which have been known and seen by the Bishop of the Diocese, and left in laymen's hands and women's too, such as he knew for good and Catholic folk, that used them with soberness and devotion." (2) But you will say, that is the witness of a Roman Catholic. Well, I shall advance Protestant testimony also.

The translators of the Authorized [i.e., "King James"] Version, in their "Preface," referring to previous translations of the Scriptures into the language of the people, make the following important statements. After speaking of the Greek and Latin versions, they proceed: "The godly-learned were not content to have the Scriptures in the language which themselves understood, Greek and Latin . . . but also for the behoof and edifying of the unlearned which hungered and thirsted after righteousness, and had souls to be saved as well as they, they provided translations into the Vulgar for their countrymen, insomuch that most nations under Heaven did shortly after their conversion hear Christ speaking unto them in their Mother tongue, not by the voice of their minister only but also by the written word translated."

Now, as all these nations were certainly converted by the Roman Catholic Church, for there was then no other to send missionaries to convert anybody, this is really a valuable admission. The Translators of 1611, then, after enumerating many converted nations that had the vernacular Scriptures, come to the case of England, and include it among the others. "Much about that time," they say (1360), "even in our King Richard the Second's days, John Trevisa translated them into English, and many English Bibles in written hand are yet to be seen that divers translated, as it is very probable, in that age. . . . So that, to have the Scriptures in the mother tongue is not a quaint conceit lately taken up, either by the Lord Cromwell in England [or others] . . . but hath been thought upon, and put in practice of old, even from

the first times of the conversion of any nation."
This testimony, from the Preface (too little known)
of their own Authorized Bible, ought surely to
carry some weight with well disposed Protestants.

Moreover, the "Reformed" Archbishop of Canterbury, Cranmer, says in his preface to the Bible
of 1540: "The Holy Bible was translated and read
in the Saxon tongue, which at that time was our
mother tongue, whereof there remaineth yet
divers copies found in old Abbeys, of such antique
manner of writing and speaking that few men
now be able to read and understand them. And
when this language waxed old and out of common
use, because folks should not lack the fruit of
reading, it was again translated into the newer
language, whereof yet also many copies remain
and be daily found." Again, Foxe, a man that
Protestants trust, says: "If histories be well exam-
ined, we shall find, both before the Conquest and
after, as well before John Wycliff was born as
since, the whole body of Scripture by sundry men
translated into our country tongue." "But as of the
earlier period, so of this, there are none but fragmentary remains, the 'many copies' which
remained when Cranmer wrote in 1540 having
doubtless disappeared in the vast and ruthless
destruction of libraries which took place within a
few years after that date." These last words are
from the pen of Rev. J. H. Blunt, a Protestant
author, in his *History of the English Bible*; and
another Anglican dignitary, Dean Hook, tells us
that "long before Wycliff's time there had been

translators of Holy Writ." One more authority on
the Protestant side, and I have done: it is Mr. Karl
Pearson (*Academy*, August, 1885), who says, "The
Catholic Church has quite enough to answer for,
but in the 15th century it certainly did not hold
back the Bible from the folk: and it gave them in
the vernacular (*i.e.*, their own tongue) a long
series of devotional works which for language and
religious sentiment have never been surpassed.
Indeed, we are inclined to think it made a mistake in allowing the masses such ready access to
the Bible. It ought to have recognized the Bible
once for all as a work absolutely unintelligible
without a long course of historical study, and, so
far as it was supposed to be inspired, very dangerous in the hands of the ignorant." We do not
know what Mr. Pearson's religious standpoint
may have been, but he goes too far in blaming the
Church for throwing the Bible open to the people
in the 15th century, or indeed in any previous age.
No evil results whatsoever followed the reading of
that precious volume in any century preceding
the 16th, because the people had the Catholic
Church to lead them and guide them and teach
them the meaning of it. It was only when the
principle of "Private Judgment" was proclaimed
that the Book became "dangerous" and "unintelligible," as it is still to the multitudes who will not
receive the true interpretation of it at the hands
of the Catholic Church, and who are about as
competent to understand and explain it by themselves as they are to explain or prophesy the

movements of the heavenly bodies.

(3) There is no need, it seems to me, to waste further time and space in accumulating proofs that the Bible was known, read and distributed by the Catholic Church in the common language of the people in all countries from the 7th down to the 14th century. I have paid more attention to the case of England because of the popularity of the myth about Wycliff having been the first to translate it and to enable the poor blinded Papists, for the first time in their experience, to behold the figure of the Christ of the Gospels in 1382. Such a grotesque notion can only be due either to ignorance or concealment of the now well-known facts of history. One would fain hope that, in this age of enlightenment and study, no one valuing his scholarship will so far imperil it as to attempt to revive the silly fable. But supposing it were as true as it is false, that John Wycliff was the first to publish the Bible in English, how in the name of reason can it be true at the same time that Luther, more than 100 years afterward, discovered it? Really, people must decide which story they are going to tell, for the one is the direct contradictory of the other. Wycliff or Luther, let it be; but Wycliff and Luther together—that is impossible.

(4) Now, it may seem somewhat irrelevant to our present subject, which is simply "where we got the Bible," to wander off to foreign lands and see how matters stood there at the date at which we have now arrived; but I should not like to pass

from this part of the inquiry without setting down a few facts which are generally unknown to our separated brethren as to the existence of plenty of Bibles in those very countries which they think were, and of course still are, plunged in the depths of superstition, illiteracy and degradation. They flatter themselves with the idea that it was the knowledge of the Scriptures which produced the blessed Reformation the world over, and will tell you that it was all because the Holy Book was sealed and locked and hidden away from the benighted Papists in Continental countries that the glorious light of the Reformation never broke, and has not yet broken, upon them. There are, however, unfortunately for them, facts at hand, facts unquestioned, which explode this pious notion. The facts are these:

(i) As was shown long ago in the *Dublin Review* (October, 1837), "It was almost solely in those countries which have remained constant to the Catholic Faith that popular versions of the Bible had been published; while it was precisely in those kingdoms, England, Scotland, Sweden, Denmark and Norway, where Protestantism acquired an early and has maintained a permanent ascendancy, that no printed Bible existed when they embraced Protestantism. Holland alone and a few cities in Germany were in possession of the Bible when they adopted the Reformed Creed." Is it really the case then, you ask with open eyes, that these Latin countries allowed the Bible to be read and translated and printed before Luther? Listen and judge for yourself what rubbish is crammed into people's heads.

(ii) Luther's first Bible (or what pretended to be the Bible, for he had amputated some of its members) came out in 1520. Now, will you believe it, there were exactly 104 editions of the Bible in Latin before that date; there were 9 before the birth of Luther in the German language, and there were 27 in German before ever his own saw the light of day. Many of these were to be seen at the Caxton Exhibition in London, 1877: and seeing is believing. In Italy there were more than 40 editions of the Bible before the first Protestant version appeared, beginning at Venice in 1471; and 25 of these were in the Italian language before 1500, with the express permission of Rome. In France there were 18 editions before 1547, the first appearing in 1478. Spain began to publish editions in the same year, and issued Bibles with the full approval of the Spanish Inquisition (of course, one can hardly expect Protestants to believe this). In Hungary by the year 1456, in Bohemia by the year 1478, in Flanders before 1500, and in other lands groaning under the yoke of Rome, we know that editions of the Sacred Scriptures had been given to the people. "In all (to quote from 'M.C.L's' useful pamphlet on the subject), 626 editions of the Bible, in which 198 were in the language of the laity, had issued from the press, with the sanction and at the instance [i.e., insistence or request] of the Church, in the countries where she reigned supreme, before the first

Protestant version of the Scriptures was sent forth into the world." England was perhaps worse off than any country at the time of the Reformation in the matter of vernacular versions of the Bible: many Catholic kingdoms abroad had far surpassed her in making known the Sacred Word. Yet these lands remained Catholic; England turned Protestant; what, then, becomes of the pathetic delusion of "Evangelical" Christians that an acquaintance with the open Bible in our own tongue must necessarily prove fatal to Catholicism? The simple truth of course is just this, that if knowledge of the Scriptures should of itself make people Protestants, then the Italian and French and Spanish and Hungarian and Belgian and Portuguese nations should all have embraced Protestantism, which up to the moment of writing they have declined to do. I am afraid there is something wrong with the theory, for it is in woeful contradiction to plain facts, which may be learned by all who care to take the trouble to read and study for themselves.

(5) Now, before passing on to another part of the subject, I should like you to pause for a moment with the brief historical review fresh in your memory; and I would simply ask this: How can anyone living in the light of modern education and history cling any longer to the fantastic idea that Rome hates the Bible—that she has done her worst to destroy it—that she conceals it from her people lest it should enlighten their blindness, and that the Holy Book, after lying for many long dark ages

in the dungeons and lumber rooms of Popery, was at last exhumed and dragged into the light of day by the great and glorious discoverer, Martin Luther? O foolish Scotchmen, who hath bewitched you? Do you not see that Rome could have easily destroyed it if she had been so disposed during all those centuries that elapsed between its formation into one volume in 397 A.D., and the sixteenth century? It was absolutely, exclusively in her power to do with it as she pleased, for Rome reigned supreme. What more simple than to order her priests and monks and Inquisitors to search out every copy and reduce it to ashes? But did she do this? We have seen that she preserved it and multiplied it. She saved it from utter destruction at the hands of infidels and barbarians and pagan tribes that burned everything Christian they could come across; she saved it and guarded it from total extinction by her care and loving watchfulness; she, and she alone. There was no one else to do it; she only was sent by God to defend His Blessed Word. It might have perished, and would have perished, were it not that she employed her clergy to reproduce it and adorn it and multiply it, and to furnish churches and monasteries with copies of it, which all might read and learn and commit to memory, and meditate upon. Nay, she not only multiplied it in its original languages (Greek and Hebrew), which would have been intelligible and useful only to the learned few, but she put it into the hands of all her people who could read, by translating it into Latin, the universal tongue; and even for those less scholarly, she rendered it into the common languages spoken in different countries. Truly she took a curious way of showing her hatred of God's Holy Word and of destroying it.

Many senseless charges are laid at the door of the Catholic Church; but surely the accusation that, during the centuries preceding the sixteenth, she was the enemy of the Bible and of Bible reading must, to anyone who does not wilfully shut his eyes to facts, appear of all accusations the most ludicrous; and to tell the truth, it is ridiculed and laughed out of court by all serious and impartial students of the question. With far more justice, it humbly seems to me, may the charge of degrading and profaning the Sacred Scriptures be brought against those highly financed Bible societies which, with a recklessness that passes comprehension, scatter among savages and pagans utterly uninstructed, tons of Testaments, only to be used for making ball cartridges or wadding; for wrapping up snuff, bacon, tobacco, fruit and other goods; for papering the walls of houses; for converting into tapestry or pretty kites for children; and for other and fouler uses which it makes one ashamed to think of. True, the versions thus degraded are false and heretical, which may mitigate the horror in the eyes of Catholics; but those who thus expose them to dishonor believe them to be the real Words of Life. On their heads, then, falls the guilt of "giving that which is holy to the dogs."

∽12∽

Why Wycliff
Was Condemned

BUT here we are likely to be met with an objection by those who have not a very profound or accurate knowledge of the history of this question. "Why, then," they will say, "why, if the Catholic Church approved of the Bible being read in the tongue of the people, why did she condemn Wycliff, one of her own priests, for translating it into English, and forbid her people to read his version of the Sacred Scriptures?" I answer, because John Wycliff's version of the Bible was not a correct version, and because he was using it as a means of corrupting the people's faith and of teaching them false doctrine; and it seems to me at least that that was a perfectly good reason for condemning it. For, please observe that while the Church approves of the people reading the Scriptures in their own language, she also claims the right to see that they really have a *true* version of the Scriptures to read, and not a mutilated or false or imperfect or heretical version. She claims that she alone has the right to make translations from the original languages (Hebrew or Greek) in which the Bible was writ-

114

ten; the right to superintend and supervise the work of translating; the right of appointing certain priests or scholars to undertake the work; the right of approving or condemning versions and translations which are submitted to her for her judgment. She declares she will not tolerate that her children should be exposed to the danger of reading copies of Scripture which have changed or falsified something of the original Apostolic writing; which have added something or left out something; which have notes and explanations and prefaces and prologues that convey false doctrine or false morals. Her people must have the correct Bible, or no Bible at all.

Rome claims that the Bible is her book; that she has preserved it and perpetuated it, and that she alone knows what it means; that nobody else has any right to it whatsoever, or any authority to declare what the true meaning of it is. She therefore has declared that the work of translating it from the original languages, and of explaining it, and of printing it and publishing it, belongs strictly to her alone; and that, if she cannot nowadays prevent those outside her fold from tampering with it and misusing it, at least she will take care that none of her own children abuse it or take liberties with it; and hence she forbids any private person to attempt to translate it into the common language without authority from ecclesiastical superiors, and also forbids the faithful to read any editions but such as are approved by the Bishops. All this the Catholic Church does out of reverence for God's Holy Word. She desires that the pure, uncorrupted Gospel should be put in her people's hands as it came from the pen of the Apostles and Evangelists. She dreads lest the faithful should draw down upon themselves a curse by believing for Gospel the additions and changes introduced by foolish and sinful men to support some pet theories of their own; just as a mother would fear lest her children should, along with water or milk, drink down some poison that was mixed up with it. There are, then, let it be clearly understood, versions *and* versions of Holy Scriptures: some that are correct and guaranteed by the Church; others that simply bristle with mistakes and falsities. The former are permitted to Catholics to read and study; the latter, it need hardly be said, are utterly forbidden. Now, to the latter class belonged the version of John Wycliff, first put into people's hands in 1382. A very slight knowledge of the man himself and of his opinions and of his career might persuade any reasonable person that a version made by him was the very last that would be allowed to Catholics.

(2) What are the simple facts about the man? He was born in 1320, became a priest and theologian and lecturer at Oxford, and at first caused notoriety by taking part with the State against the claims of the Pope in regard to tribute money and benefices. But in the course of a few years he went further and began to oppose the Church not only in matters of policy or government (a course which might conceivably at times be pardonable),

but in the things of faith. Being accused of preaching novel and uncommon doctrines, he was, at the instance of Pope Gregory XI, summoned before his Archbishop in 1378 and inhibited from teaching any further on the matters in dispute. No more proceedings were taken against him (though he did not desist from his anti-Papal teaching) till 1381, when again he was making himself notorious. He attacked the friars and religious orders with great bitterness, impugned Transubstantiation, and seemed to advocate the theory that was afterwards peculiarly Luther's, ridiculed indulgences and flooded the country with pamphlets and tracts reeking with heresy. He was, in short, a kind of Lollard. "The Lollards" (says the *National Cyclopædia*) "were a religious sect which rose in Germany at the beginning of the fourteenth century, and differed in many points of doctrine from the Church of Rome, more especially as regards the Mass, Extreme Unction, and atonement for sin."

That, of course, is a very bald and crude statement of their tenets. The extent of their "differences from the Church of Rome" will appear in a clearer light if we consider the "Lollards' Petition to Parliament," 1395. It contained among other novelties the famous "twelve conclusions" against the temporal possessions of the Church, the celibacy of the clergy, and all vows of chastity; against exorcisms and blessings of inanimate objects; Transubstantiation and prayers for the dead; pilgrimages; compulsory auricular confession; veneration of images; and the holding of secular offices by priests. Many also objected to the taking of oaths, denied the necessity of Baptism for salvation, held marriage to be a mere civil contract and spoke of sacramentals as "jugglery." (See *Chambers Cyclopædia* and *The Catholic Cyclopædia*, under "Lollards.") Now, you may sympathize with these amiable persons if you like, but you would hardly expect the Catholic Church of that century (or of any century) to sympathize with them, and still less to suffer them to issue her Scriptures expurgated according to their ideas. But thus did John Wycliff. "He held views" (says the devout Anglican, Doré, in his most interesting work, *Old Bibles*)—"he held views which, if carried into practice, would have been totally subversive of morality and good order, but he never separated himself from the [Catholic] Church of England." Another Anglican says the Lollards were political martyrs rather than religious; that their actions tended to a Revolution in the state as well as in the Church; and that both civilians and ecclesiastics regarded their principles as subversive of all order in things temporal as well as things spiritual. (Dr. Hook, *Lives of Archbishops of Canterbury*). Can we be surprised, then, at reading that in 1382, in consequence of the monstrous heresies that he was now spreading, John Wycliff was again put on trial by the ecclesiastical courts and that 22 propositions taken from his works were condemned? Thereupon he retired to Lutterworth, of which he had been Rector for many years. He was gently dealt with, and his declining years were not harassed by any of the persecution and torture which it pleases some to depict him as suffering; and he died, after a stroke of paralysis while hearing Mass, on the 31st of December, 1384. In later years, two separate Councils, one at London, the other at Constance, selected 45 propositions from the teaching of Wycliff and condemned them, declaring some to be notoriously heretical; others erroneous; others scandalous and blasphemous; others seditious and rash; and the rest offensive to pious ears.

(3) Now, I ask any unprejudiced person, was this the kind of man to undertake the translation of the Bible into the common language of the people? Was he likely to be trusted by the Church at that time to produce a version thoroughly Catholic and free from all error or corruption—a man notoriously eccentric, guilty of heretical and suspicious teaching, attacking the Church in its authorities from the Pope down to the friars, and associated with sectaries abroad who were at once revolutionaries and heretics? The question answers itself. You may cry out that Wycliff was right and Rome was wrong in doctrine; that he was a glorious Reformer and "morning star of the Reformation," and that he taught the pure word of the Lord as against the abominable traditions of the Scarlet Woman of Babylon. But I humbly submit that that is not the point. The point is this: you ask why did the Catholic Church condemn Wycliff's version and at the same time allow other

versions of the Bible in English, and I am showing you why. I am telling you that Wycliff was
heretical in the eyes of Rome; that he produced a
heretical version for the purpose of attacking the
Catholic Church of that day, and of spreading his
heresies; and that to blame the Church for forbidding him to do so, and for condemning his version,
is about as sensible as to blame an author for
interdicting someone else from publishing a copy
of his work that was full of errors and absurdities,
and contained opinions and sentiments which he
detested. The Catholic Church certainly could
never allow a version of Holy Scripture (which is
her own book) like that of Wycliff to go forth
unchallenged, as if it were correct and authoritative and bore her sanction and approval. As well
might we expect the British Sovereign to sanction
some hideous caricature from a comic paper as a
true and faithful picture of his coronation.

(4) We do not shrink from giving John Wycliff
and Nicholas of Hereford an equal share of praise
for their laborious work of translating the whole
of the Bible into the English tongue, if the work
was really theirs (which some scholars like Gasquet, however, have doubted). What we assert is
that it was a bad translation, and hence useless,
and worse than useless, for Catholics. It was condemned and forbidden to be used by a Decree of
Archbishop Arundel at Oxford in 1408, which also
prohibited the translation of any part of the Bible
into English by any unauthorized person, and the
reading of any version before it was formally

approved. This was a natural and wise and necessary decree. It did not forbid the reading of any of the *old approved versions* of Scripture in English which existed in great numbers before Wycliff, as we have seen already. Nor did it forbid new versions to be made or read, if under proper supervision and approval by ecclesiastical superiors. It only banned false and unauthorized translations like Wycliff's; and Protestant writers, like Dr. Hook, have often declared their belief that it was not from hostility to a translated Bible as such that the Church condemned Wycliff, and that she never would have issued her decree if his sole purpose had been the edification and sanctification of the readers. It was only when the design of the Lollards was discovered, and Wycliff's subtle plot unmasked of disseminating their pestilential errors through his translation, that the Church's condemnation fell upon him. A greater authority even than Dr. Hook—I mean the veteran historian, Dr. James Gairdner, an English Churchman who spent more than 60 of his fourscore years in research among the State papers of England dealing with the period about the Reformation, and who was recognized as easily the most profound and comprehensive student of those times—Dr. Gairdner, I say, expressed some very strong conclusions, to which his historical inquiries had driven him, in regard to the Wycliffite revolt and its results, and about Rome and the Bible. (See his book *Lollardy and the Reformation*, reviewed in *Month*, December, 1908.) "The truth is," he says,

"the Church of Rome was not at all opposed to the
making of translations of Scripture or to placing
them in the hands of the laity under what were
deemed proper precautions. It was only judged
necessary to see that no unauthorized or corrupt
translations got abroad; and even in this matter,
it would seem the authorities were not roused to
special vigilance till they took alarm at the diffu-
sion of Wycliffite translations in the generation
after his death." (Vol. I, p. 105). Again: "To the possession by worthy lay men of licensed translations the Church was never opposed; but to place
such a weapon as an English Bible in the hands
of men who had no regard for authority, and who
would use it without being instructed how to use
it properly, was dangerous not only to the souls of
those who read, but to the peace and order of the
Church." (P. 117). From a deep, calm scholar like
Dr. Gairdner, words like these are more valuable
than whole volumes of partisan and unenlight-
ened assertions from anti-Catholic controversial-
ists; and (as Father Thurston suggests) we cannot
but feel grateful to this honored old scholar in the
evening of his days for thus vigorously and boldly
identifying himself with an unpopular cause.
Simply, honesty of purpose and love of truth compelled him, out of his vast and prolonged studies,
to expose the revolutionary character of the
Wycliffite and Lollard rebellions against Rome, as
well as to sympathize with the glorious martyrs
like More and Fisher, and to defend the Catholic
authorities like Archbishop Warham and Bishops

Bonner and Tunstall, and to vindicate the good reputation and piety of the monasteries so cruelly suppressed by Henry VIII. But we are anticipating. I was speaking of the Church's condemnation of Wycliff's undesired and undesirable version.

(5) This was the first time in England that the Church ever felt herself obliged to lay some restriction on Bible reading in the vulgar tongue [vernacular]; and that fact in itself is surely sufficient to prove that there must have been some very special reason for her acting so differently from what she had been accustomed to do before. Her action at this time was precisely similar to the action of the Church in France nearly 200 years previously. Then (that is, in the 12th and 13th centuries), some heretics called Waldenses and Albigenses revolted against all authority and overran the country, spreading their wild and blasphemous doctrines. They taught, among other enormities, that there were two Gods (creator of the good and creator of the evil), that there was no Real Presence of Our Lord in the Blessed Eucharist, that there was no forgiveness for sins after Baptism, and that there was no resurrection of the body. They declared oaths unlawful, condemned marriage, and called the begetting of children a crime. All these impieties they professed to base on Holy Scripture. Consequently, to save her people from being ensnared and led away, the Church in council assembled at Toulouse, 1229, passed an enactment forbidding to laymen the possession of the sacred books, especially in the

vernacular, though anyone might possess a Bre-
viary or a Psalter or Office of our Blessed Lady for
devotion. Will anyone blame the Church for taking
these measures to suppress the poisonous heresy
and prevent its spreading, and to save the Sacred
Scriptures from being made the mere tool and war
cry of a certain sect? In like manner, we may not
blame the Church at Oxford under Archbishop
Arundel for her famous constitution against
Wycliffite and other false versions of the Bible, but
rather admire and applaud her wisdom and vigilance and zeal for the purity of the Gospel of Jesus
Christ. And in the same way we may examine and
investigate the action of the Church in various
countries and in various centuries as to her legislation in regard to Bible reading among the people; and wherever we find some apparently severe
or unaccountable prohibition of it, we shall on
inquiry find that it was necessitated by the foolish
or sinful conduct on the part either of some of her
own people, or of bitter and aggressive enemies
who literally forced her to forbid what in ordinary
circumstances she would not only have allowed
but have approved and encouraged.

It is true that the approving or condemning of
Bible reading in particular centuries or countries
is a matter of policy and of discipline on the part
of the local Catholic authorities, and depends
largely upon the prudence and wisdom and zeal of
the Bishops set over them, and does not necessarily involve any action on the part of the Pope as
Supreme Head of the Church; and hence one can-

not declare infallibly off-hand that there has never been a case of unwise or indiscreet legislation in regard to the matter at the hands of individual Bishops. I do not know of any case myself and never read of any instance where Bishops have been proved in the course of time to have made mistakes in issuing decrees about the matter. But supposing some mistake had been made, that would not affect the general principle on which the ecclesiastical authorities always are supposed to act; and in the light of Rome's principle, and her clear and definite attitude toward the Bible as her own Book, we may safely challenge anyone to convict her either of inconsistency or hatred toward God's written Word. Once grasp her doctrinal position in regard to the Bible and the Rule of Faith, and you will have no difficulty in accounting for her uncompromising hostility to versions like Wycliff's, and for her action in condemning the Bible Societies which spread abroad a mutilated, corrupt and incomplete copy of the Holy Scriptures (generally accompanied by tracts) with the design of undermining the faith of Catholics.

∽13∽

Tyndale's Condemnation Vindicated by Posterity

SO much then for John Wycliff and his unhappy version. The next man of any consequence we are confronted with is another favorite of the Reformers, another "martyr" for the Bible, and that is William Tyndale. His treatment is also flung in our teeth by critics as fresh evidence of Rome's implacable hatred of the open Bible. Did she not persecute and burn poor Tyndale and consign his copy of the Scriptures in English to the flames? So here again, we must show how wise and consistent was the action of the Catholic Church in England in regard to Tyndale and his translations, and clear her absolutely from the slightest shadow or suspicion of hostility to God's written Word.

(i) What we are about to speak of now, be it remembered, is the printed Bible, for in 1450 the art of printing was discovered by a man rejoicing in the melodious name of John Gooseflesh (a German), and in 1456 the first book ever printed issued from the press at Mayence, and it was—what? It was the Bible, and it is known as the Mazarin Bible, after Cardinal Mazarin. This again demonstrates anew what hatred Catholics had in those days to the Bible, and their fear and dread lest it should be known even to exist! The best way to keep it secret, of course, was to print it. Besides, how could the Bible be printed in 1456? Did not Martin Luther discover it for the first time in 1507? However, joking apart, the fact remains that we have now in our historical review arrived at the point where we bid farewell to copies of the Bible written by the hand and have to consider only those that were turned out by the printing press from 1456 onward. On Protestant principles it must seem a pity that the Lord waited so many centuries before He invented printing machines to spread Bibles about among the people; and it seems also very hard on all preceding generations that slipped away without this lamp to their feet and light unto their path.

(ii) Well, William Tyndale (and, for that matter, Martin Luther too) was born almost 100 years after John Wycliff died, that is, 1484. He studied at Oxford and became a priest, and was seized with the ambition of getting the Bible printed in England. Now, there were three great objections to this step being approved. (1) In the first place, Tyndale was not the man to do it; he was utterly unfitted for such a great work. He says himself he was "evil favoured in this world, and without grace in the sight of men, speechless and rude, dull and slow witted." He had no special qualifications for the task of translation. He was but a mediocre scholar, and could not boast of anything above the average intellect. Indeed, non-Catholic authors have admitted that the cause of Scripture reading in the vernacular was distinctly prejudiced by having been taken in hand by incapable men like Tyndale. (2) Then, in the second place, he was acting entirely on his own account, and without authorization from ecclesiastical superiors, either in England or in Rome; he was simply a private obscure priest and was acting without commission and without sanction from higher quarters. Indeed, I go further and say that he was acting in disobedience to the decision of higher authorities. At the very beginning of the sixteenth century (I am now quoting the Anglican Doré), "the authorities of the English [Catholic] Church took into consideration the desirability of introducing a vernacular Bible [*i.e.,* Bible in English] into England, and the great majority of the Council were of opinion that, considering the religious troubles on the Continent and the unsettled state of things at home, at this juncture the translation of the Bible into the vulgar tongue, and its circulation among the people, would rather tend to confusion and distraction than to edification." Now, you may lament if you like (as Doré does) this decision as an error of judgment, and affirm that the postponement of an English version in print authorized by the Bishops was a most unfortunate event, as leading to false and corrupt versions being issued by irresponsible individuals. But right or wrong in their judgment, this was the conscientious conclusion at which the Council under Archbishop Wareham arrived: no printed English Bible meanwhile was to be allowed; and after all is said and done, they were probably better judges than we are as to what was best for the Church of that time in England. The Lutheran Revolution was in full swing abroad (1520), and the Lutheran heresy was spreading everywhere, carrying with it rebellion and immorality, and the English Bishops might well have cause to fear lest the infection should poison the faithful under their own jurisdiction. (3) In the third place, there was no demand for a printed English Bible to any great extent—certainly not to the extent of making it at all an urgent or pressing duty on the part of the authorities to issue one. Doré (so often quoted already) ridicules the idea that at that time England was a "Bible-thirsty land." He declares that "there was no anxiety whatever for an English version excepting among a small minority of the people," and "the universal desire for a Bible in England we read so much of in most works on the subject existed only in the imagination of the writers." Dr. Brewer, another Protestant, also scoffs at the idea. "To imagine," he says, "that ploughmen and shepherds in the country read the New Testament in English by stealth, or that smiths and carpenters in towns pored over its pages in the corner of their masters' workshops, is to mistake the character and acquirements of the age." There has, in short, been a great deal of wild and groundless talk about the intense desire of the people of that century to devour the Scriptures. And we can prove it by these simple facts, that (1) the people had to be compelled by law to buy Bibles, for Acts were passed again and again threatening the King's displeasure and a fine of 40s.* per month if the Book was not purchased; (2) we have documentary evidence that inhabitants of certain parts of the country, such as Cornwall and Devonshire, unanimously objected to the new translation, and that even among the clergy, Reformers like Bishop Hugh Latimer almost entirely ignored the English copy and always took their texts from the Latin Vulgate; (3) printers had large stocks of printed Bibles left unsold on their hands, and could not get rid of them at any price, except under legal coercion; (4) the same edition of the Bible was often re-issued with fresh titles and preliminary matter; and new title pages were composed for old unsold Bibles, without any regard to truth, simply to get them sold. I do not see how we can resist the conviction that there was really no extensive demand for English Bibles among the mass of Christians at that time in England, whether clergy or laity, and that the design of spreading them wholesale among the masses was borrowed from the Continent, which was then in a perfect ferment of religious and civil

---

*40s. = 40 shillings or, very roughly, $1,000 today. (A shilling = 1/20 of a British £.) See footnote on p. 78. —*Publisher*, 2004.

revolution. Hence you can understand at once how Tyndale's proposal was viewed with suspicion and disfavor by the Bishops, and himself refused any assistance or encouragement from Tunstall, Bishop of London, and other prelates. And when we further bear in mind (as the *Athenæum* pertinently remarked, 24th August, 1889) that this irresponsible private chaplain had become already known as a man of dangerous views, who was exceedingly insulting in his manner, unscrupulous, and of a most violent temper; that in postprandial discussions he repeatedly abused and insulted Church dignitaries who were present; that with him the Pope was anti-Christ and the whore of Babylon, while the monks and friars were "caterpillars, horseleeches, drone-bees, and draff," we shall not be vastly astonished that these dignitaries did not evince much enthusiasm in pushing on Mr. Tyndale's scheme.

(iii) Unable therefore to proceed with the work in his own land because of ecclesiastical prohibition, Tyndale goes abroad, and after much wandering about settles at Worms, where in 1525 the Bible was printed and thence smuggled in considerable quantities into England. At once, as was to be expected, it was denounced by the Bishop of London, and I do not deny (nor can I see any reason to deplore) the fact that copies of it were burned ceremonially at St. Paul's Cross. But why? Because it was a false and erroneous and anti-Catholic version of the Holy Scriptures. It was full of Lutheran heresies. Tyndale had fallen under the influence of the German Reformer, who by this time had revolted from Rome. About 1522 he had been suspected and tried for heresy; he had declared: "I defy the Pope and all his laws;" and now he actually embodied in his English version Luther's notes and explanations of texts, which were as full of venom and hatred against Rome as an egg is full of meat [i.e., food]. "It has long been a notorious fact," says Mr. Allnatt (in his *Bible and the Reformation*), "that all the early Protestant versions of the Bible literally swarmed with gross and flagrant corruptions—corruptions consisting in the wilful and deliberate mistranslation of various passages of the sacred text, and all directly aimed against those doctrines and practices of the Catholic Church which the 'Reformers' were most anxious to uproot. They did give the people an 'open Bible,' but what a Bible!" And Canon Dixon, the cultured Anglican historian, referring to the fact that copies of Tyndale's Bible were burned, makes these striking remarks: "If the clergy had acted thus simply because they would have the people kept ignorant of the Word of God, they would have been without excuse. But it was not so. Every one of the little volumes containing portions of the sacred text that was issued by Tyndale contained also a prologue and notes written with such hot fury of vituperation against the prelates and clergy, the monks and friars, the rites and ceremonies of the Church, as was hardly likely to commend it to the favor of those who were attacked." Tunstall, Bishop of London, declared he could count more than 2,000 errors in Tyndale's Bible "made in Germany"; while the learned Sir Thomas More, Lord Chancellor of England, found it necessary to write a treatise against it, and asserted that to "find errors in Tyndale's book were like studying to find water in the sea." In short, there is not an unprejudiced inquirer now but admits that the Church could not possibly tolerate Tyndale's Bible as though it were a true or correct version of the Holy Scriptures; she had no alternative but to prescribe and forbid it; otherwise she would have been sinfully neglectful of her guardianship over the Word of God, and idly standing by while her children were being poisoned. But who will be so obtuse or so malicious as to twist this action of hers into a determined hatred of the Scriptures *as Scriptures* and to represent her as hostile and opposed to all reading of the Bible whatsoever, even of a true and correct version? Surely to hate the Bible is one thing, and to prohibit a false version of the Bible is quite another. Has the Catholic Church not as a matter of fact put a correct copy of the Bible into the hands of her children in their own language in the Douay version? As for the burning of Tyndale's version, there is nothing to be wondered at in it; it was probably the only, or at least the most striking and effective way of stemming its sale and instilling a horror of it into the hearts of the people. It was the custom of the age (as Doré remarks) to burn the works of opponents, as Luther a few years before burned the books of Canon Law and the Bull of Pope Leo, and in 1522 John Calvin burned all the copies he could collect of Servetus' Bible at Geneva, because these contained some notes he did not think were orthodox. Indeed, Calvin went a step further than that—he burned Servetus himself. And surely it must be plain enough to everyone that, in the case before us, what the ecclesiastical authorities meant to destroy was, not the Word of God, but the errors of Luther and Tyndale which were corrupting it.

(iv) But the most interesting point about the whole affair is that time has abundantly justified the action of the Catholic Church and proved that she did the proper thing in attempting to stamp out Tyndale's Bible. For (1) the reading of this pernicious book produced most disastrous effects upon the morals of the people, who became rebellious, profane and irreligious, and disaffected to the civil as well as to the spiritual authorities. Hence we find that for ten years, Tyndale's version was denounced and opposed even more by the Court and secular officials than by the Bishops; and that at least two royal proclamations were issued for every one clerical against all who read or concealed the obnoxious volume. In fact, in the year 1531 King Henry VIII, with the advice of his Council and prelates, published an edict that the translation of the Scripture corrupted by William Tyndale should be utterly expelled, rejected, and put away out of the hands of the people, and not be suffered to go abroad among his subjects. What a commentary upon the good and godly doctrines inculcated by Mr. William Tyndale! And further still—some years later (the King's veto not having secured the desired effect), after several other editions of the English Bible had been issued and the condition of the Scripture-reading masses was becoming worse and worse in consequence, the same Royal Defender of the Faith caused another Act to be passed (1543) entitled "for the advancement of true religion and for the abolishment of the contrary." By force of this it was decreed that, seeing what abuses had followed the indiscriminate reading of certain versions of Holy Scripture, and what "tumults and schisms" had sprung up, and "divers naughty and erroneous opinions," and "pestiferous and noisome teachings and instructions" including "writings against the holy and blessed Sacrament of the Altar, and for the maintenance of the damnable opinions of the sect of Anabaptists"— all to the "great unquietness of the realm and great displeasure of his Majesty" as a result of all this, it was enacted that "all manner of books of the Old and New Testament in English, being of the *crafty, false, and untrue translation of Tyndale*," along with any writings containing doctrine contrary to that of the King, "shall be clearly and utterly abolished, extinguished, and forbidden to be kept or used in this realm." The Act then goes on to explain what versions of the Bible might be used, and by whom, and forbids the general reading of it by women, artificers, journeymen and certain other classes, and lays down sundry other restrictions in regard to it which are to be observed under pains and penalties ranging from fines of 40s. and £5 and £40 up to imprisonment for life. I shall not dwell on the reflections that arise in one's mind on reading such legal enactments coming from such a man as Henry VIII; but, to complete our remarks about Tyndale's version and to pursue to the end the King's dealing with it, I may add that the very year (1546) before he went to his account he struck one more blow, which no doubt he intended to be and hoped would be fatal, at this hated volume. He deliberately commanded all copies of it (along with Coverdale's) to be delivered up and burned. Verily the "whirligig of time brings in his revenges." After this, one finds it somewhat amusing to be told that only priests and Popes burn and hate the Word of God. Henceforth Protestant readers of these lines would do well to remember that the great Reformer and Founder of the Church of England, Henry VIII, set a high example in the matter. However, that is by the way. I was saying that the time justified the action of the Church which first proscribed and did its utmost to repress Tyndale's version, and I have shown how the secular power felt itself driven in self-protection to do the same. (2) But another, and perhaps to Protestants a more telling proof of the statement is found in the fact that their subsequent versions of Scripture deliberately omitted Tyndale's most characteristic features, such as his notes, prefaces and prologues. They appeared and then they disappeared. They had their day, and they ceased to be. They were considered unfit to find a place in what purported to be a pure copy of the work of the Apostle and Evangelist. Posterity, then, has justified Sir [now Saint] Thomas More and has condemned Tyndale. What is this but to vindicate the Church in her action toward the corrupt volume? Wisdom is indeed "justified of her children."

∽14∽

A Deluge
Of Erroneous Versions

FOLLOWING Tyndale's example, others continued the work of issuing English-printed Bibles, and so in the reign of Henry VIII we have to face quite a deluge of them. One by one they came forth, authorized and unauthorized, printed and published by irresponsible individuals, full of errors, with no proper supervision, and having no other effect (as we shall presently see) than that of drawing down contempt and disgrace upon the Sacred Scriptures.

(1) The English Church was now separated from Rome, and the English Bishops were mere puppets and slaves at the beck and call of the Royal Tyrant, Henry. They exercised no real independent jurisdiction over either clergy or people; the governor and ruler in Church and State was the King; and consequently no ecclesiastic could undertake responsibility in regard to the publication or suppression of Bibles without the will of his Imperial Master. So long as Henry made no objection, any printer or publisher or literary hack who thought he saw a chance of making a

little money out of the venture would take in hand the publishing of a new version of the Bible. George Joye, for example, took this course in regard to Tyndale's Bible, and in consequence (1535) brought down upon himself a volley of bitter and un-Christian reproaches from that worthy, who (as I have said before) was a man of uncontrollable temper and scurrilous language when thwarted or resisted. In reply to this tirade, George Joye published an "Apology" in which he showed that the printer had paid him only 4½d. for the correction of every 16 leaves, while Tyndale had netted £10 for his work; and besides, he exposed in fine style the departure from the truth of which Tyndale had been guilty in boasting of his translation and exposition as if it were his own, whereas Joye shows it was really Luther's all the time; that Tyndale did not know enough Greek to do it, and had only added "fantasies" and glosses and notes of his own imagination to the work of others. However, we have no time to dwell on the quarrels of these amiable Bible translators, else we should never reach the end of our historical review. Let us enumerate briefly the versions that saw the light in rapid succession during the reign of Henry VIII.

(2) There was Myles Coverdale's in 1535. Coverdale was a priest who married abroad and kept a school. In after years King Edward VI granted him and his wife (sic) Elizabeth a dispensation (!) to eat flesh and white meats in Lent and other fasting days. It is wonderful what power the

Kings of England had in those days! In 1537 appeared Matthew's or Rogers' Bible (which was a mixture of Tyndale's and Coverdale's), and this has the distinction of being the first that Henry authorized to be used by the people at large. Matthew or Rogers (for he assumed different names for Bible-selling purposes) was, like Coverdale, a renegade priest, and had married, and we are not surprised to find that some of his notes on the Gospel were indecent, and others consisted of abuse of the Church, her clergy and her doctrines. Two years later (1539) a man, Taverner, produced another version of the Bible. He was a layman, but a preacher notwithstanding, who had saved his skin by recanting his opinions. And the same year appeared a version that was to hold the field for popularity for the next twenty years, namely, the Great Bible, sometimes called Cranmer's, from the Preface written by that accommodating prelate. It was Cromwell (Thomas, not Oliver, of course) who engineered it, and Coverdale who supervised its progress. The printing of it was begun in France, but when the work was half finished, the Inquisitor-General very properly stepped in and confiscated the presses and types. If England was going to the dogs through anti-Papal Bibles, he saw no reason why France should do the same. However, it was completed and published in London in 1539, and, like previous versions, contained fulsome flattery of Henry VIII, concerning whom Our Lord is represented as saying, "I have found a man after My

Own heart, who shall fulfill all My will!" This volume was by Royal Proclamation ordered to be put up in every church in England; and Bonner, Bishop of London ("Bloody Bonner"), who is held up as the most determined enemy of Bible reading, set up at his own expense six beautiful copies of this Book at various convenient places in St. Paul's Cathedral. Unfortunately, so much ill-feeling, disturbance, contention and irreverence was the result of this unrestrained Scripture reading that he was compelled to threaten their removal. The license to read and judge, each one for himself, of the sense and meaning of the Word of God produced, as we said before, most lamentable effects, and led to the utter degradation of the Sacred Volume. Not that there was any eager desire or thirst for it, or any great or general use made of it: for the printers often complained of the large stock left, unbought, on their hands, and begged that persons should be compelled to purchase them, and besought that no fresh editions might be published; and we have seen that Acts had to be made to force people to buy them, under threat of fine and imprisonment. But yet those who did read the Bible made it only a matter of altercation and contention and argument, and brought it down to the depths of disrepute and contempt. The extent to which this evil had spread may best be judged from the pathetic lament of Henry VIII himself in his last speech to Parliament: "I am extremely sorry to find how much the Word of God is abused: with how little reverence it is mentioned; how people squabble about the sense; how it is turned into wretched rhymes, sung and jangled in every alehouse and tavern; and all this in a false construction and counter-meaning to the inspired writers. I am sorry to perceive the readers of the Bible discover so little of it in their practice; for I am sure charity was never in a more languishing condition, virtue never at a lower ebb, nor God Himself less honored or worse served in Christendom." There is no ambiguity about these words, and when we remember that the same sentiments are expressed in the writings and speeches of many of the Reformers themselves, who complain of the licentiousness of the masses since the abolition of Popery, and remember, too, how Henry VIII was constrained to seize and burn Tyndale's and Coverdale's and other versions of the Bible, and to forbid the reading of any version at all to large classes of his subjects—in the face of all this, who will fail to see the sinful folly of the policy of the English schismatics of that day? And who will deny that the Catholic Church showed consummate wisdom, holy prudence and the truest reverence for God's Word in withholding her version till a more convenient season?

(3) But are we finished with the erroneous versions yet? Far from it. Henry VIII certainly authorized no more, for the simple reason that he went to Judgment in 1547. No new edition came out in Edward VI's reign (1547-1553), but in 1557 one was published that owed its origin to William

Whittingham, a layman, who had married a sister of John Calvin's wife, and who was made Dean of Durham. Whittingham's Bible, issued at Geneva, perpetuated the corruptions of Tyndale's with an Epistle of Calvin added to the Epistles of St. Paul and the other Apostles. During the reign of "Bloody" Mary (1553-1558), who, of course, ought to have hated the Scriptures like poison (being a bigoted Papist and the wife of a Spaniard), there were, strange to say, no proclamations against Scripture reading, nor is there to be found any trace of opposition on the part either of the Queen or of her Bishops to the Bible being read or printed in the vulgar tongue; so says Mr. Blunt, the Anglican historian. With the accession of the "Virgin Queen Bess," however, a new Bible saw the light in 1560 at Geneva, which was the work of the Nonconformists resident there, and is known as the Genevan Bible, though Bible collectors know it more familiarly by the title "Breeches Bible," from its rendering of Genesis 3:7: "They sewed fig leaves together and made themselves breeches." It was certainly the most popular that had yet appeared among the sectaries, partly because of its undeniable scholarship and accuracy, and partly because of its notes on the margin, which were fiercely Calvinistic. Take an example: Revelations 9:3. Here the note runs: "Locusts are false teachers, heretics and wordly subtil prelates, with monks, friars, cardinals, patriarchs, archbishops, bishops, doctors, bachelors, masters, which forsake Christ to maintain false doctrine." Nobody worth speaking about is missed out here.

The Puritan soldiers used to carry about with them a little book made up of quotations from the notes of this Calvinistic version. It seems also to have suited the Scottish taste of the period, for it was the first edition printed in Scotland. So little, however, did the great mass of the people in this country care for any Bible in English at all that the Privy Council passed a law compelling every householder possessed of a certain sum to purchase a copy under a penalty of £10. The Magistrates and Town Council of Edinburgh also did their best to force the sale of the volume; and searchers went from house to house throughout this unhappy land to see if it had been bought. But, in spite of all the pressure, we find from the Privy Council records that many householders preferred to incur the pains and penalties to purchasing the Bible. The old dodge was then adopted in regard to the Genevan version that had done service with previous copies—the dodge, namely, of issuing the very same book, with the same errors and identical notes, but under a new title page, so as to deceive the unwary into believing it was a fresh edition. This trick had to be played, of course, by the unfortunate and impecunious printers and booksellers, who had large stocks of Bibles unsold on their shelves; and the perpetration of this fraud helped the Genevan editions considerably. But the Elizabethan Bishops soon found that this Bible, with its violent

Calvinistic notes and teaching, was undermining the popularity of the Church of England; so Matthew Parker, Archbishop of Canterbury, set himself the task of providing another version that would be less offensive to the High Church party and more favorable to Anglicanism. The result was the Bishops' Bible, which appeared in 1568, and took the chief place in the public services of the Church, though it never displaced the Genevan in the favor of the people.

We are close now to the moment at which the first Catholic version (and up till today [i.e., 1911] the only one ever sanctioned in English) appeared. But there was still one more Protestant version which, as it is yet the principal recognized Bible of the Protestants of the British Empire, must not be omitted. I mean, of course, King James's version of 1611. It is the 300th anniversary of this, commonly called the Authorized Version, that English-speaking Protestants are everywhere celebrating this year (1911).

(4) Neither the Royal pedant himself, nor anybody else, seems to have been satisfied with any of the Bibles then floating about. Dr. Reynolds, the Puritan leader, "moved his Majesty there might be a new translation of the Bible, because those which were allowed in the reign of Henry VIII and Edward VI were corrupt, and not answerable to the truths of the original." James, great scholar as he thought himself to be, professed "that he could never yet see a Bible well translated into English, but the worst of all his

Majesty thought the Geneva"—a judgment we cannot be surprised at, considering that that version openly allowed disobedience to a king, and blamed Asa for only deposing his mother and not killing her. (*2 Chron.* 15:16). Moreover, he declared that "some of its notes were very partial, untrue, seditious, and savoured too much of dangerous and traitorous conceits." Hence a large band of translators was appointed, and in 1611 there was finished and published what has proved to be the best Protestant version that ever appeared—one which has exercised an enormous influence not only on the minds of its readers, but also on English literature throughout the world. In 1881-1885 this version of King James was revised, but while acceptable to students, the Revision has gained no hold upon the people at large.

(5) How long it will be before another Protestant version appears, he would be a bold man who would venture to prophesy; but that others will spring up and add to the number of the wrecks that already strew the path we may confidently predict. I have given a goodly list of corrupt and erroneous versions; but please do not imagine for a moment that my catalogue is anything like complete. I have merely mentioned those that were more commonly used and secured a certain amount of popularity and authorization from Protestant headquarters. But there are, I am safe in saying, hundreds of other editions that flooded this unhappy realm from the time of Tyndale—

some from foreign countries, like Holland and Germany and Switzerland, and some produced at home, but all of them swarming with blunders and perversions. On glancing over a bookseller's catalogue the other day, my eye happened to light on some of those that have attained notoriety for their absurd mistakes. There is, for example, the "He" Bible and the "She" Bible, so called from the hopeless mixing up of these pronouns in the Book of Ruth; the "He" Bible has one set of errors and the "She" Bible another. There is the "Wicked" Bible from the word "not" being omitted from the 7th Commandment. There is the "Vinegar" Bible, from printing "vinegar" instead of "vineyard," and so producing "The Parable of the Vinegar." This Bible was printed by a man called Baskett, and is now vainly sought for by collectors on account of its numberless errors; indeed, it was wittily called the "Basket-ful of Errors." There is the "Murderer's Bible," from the words of Our Lord being thus printed: "But Jesus said unto her, let the children first be killed" (instead of "fed"). Then we have the "Whig" Bible and the "Unrighteous" Bible and the "Bug" Bible and the "Treacle" Bible, and no end of other kinds of Bibles, all crammed full of mistakes and corruptions. The Pearl Bible, for instance, published by Field, the Parliamentary printer, has 6,000 errors in it. A famous book was written by a man named Ward in the seventeenth century entitled *Errata of the Protestant Bible*, containing a formidable list of—I should not like to say how many thousand errors, in the various versions. No one has yet succeeded in refuting Ward's *Errata*. It stands as a gruesome commentary on the history of heretical treatment of the inspired text. I came across a curious and rare book one day in Glasgow University Library, written in 1659 by a Protestant, one William Kilburn, entitled *Dangerous Errors in Several Late Printed Bibles to the Great Scandal and Corruption of Sound and True Religion*. He enumerates the errors, omissions and specimens of nonsense that he discovered in these editions, many of them imported from Holland, and mentions that a gentleman had unearthed 6,000 mistakes in one copy alone.

(6) But time would fail to tell of all the corruptions and perversions of the original texts which are to be found in practically all the Protestant Bibles, down to the present time, and whose existence is proved by the fact that one after the other has been withdrawn, and its place taken by a fresh version, which in its turn was found to be no better than the rest. Is this reverence for the Word of God? Which of all these corrupt partisan versions was "the Rule of Faith?" The Bible, and the Bible only, we are told; but which Bible? I ask. Or had Protestants a different Rule of Faith according to the century in which they lived? According to the copy of the Bible they chanced to possess? What a mockery of Religion! What a degradation of God's Holy Word, that it should have been knocked about like a shuttlecock and made to serve the interests now of this sect, now

of that, and loaded with notes that shrieked aloud party war cries and bitter accusations and filthy insinuations! Is this zeal for the pure and incorrupt Gospel? Is this the grand and unspeakable blessing of the "open Bible"? It only remains now to show by contrast the calm, dignified and reverent action taken by the Catholic Church toward her own Book.

The Catholic's Bible (Douay)

W HAT was the Catholic Church doing all this time? Well, she was in a state of persecution in England, and could not do very much except suffer.

(1) Many of her best sons went abroad to more favorable lands. The circumstances had assuredly been most unsuitable for bringing out a Catholic version of the Scriptures. She was rather content, indeed compelled, to sit still and from her majestic height look down and watch the rise and fall, the publication and withdrawal, the appearance and disappearance of dozens of different versions, heretical and corrupt, grotesque in their blunders and bitter in their sectarianism, that had been issued by the various bodies. By the end of the 16th century no less than 270 new sects had been enumerated, and some that had been extinct for centuries, like Arianism, revived under the genial influence of Luther. Dr. Walton, Bishop of Chester and author of the famous Polyglott Bible that bears his name, laments this fact in his Preface about the end of the 17th century. "There is no fanatic or clown," says he, "from the lowest dregs of the people who does not give you his own

dreams as the Word of God. For the bottomless pit seems to have been set open, from whence a smoke has risen which has obscured the heavens and the stars, and locusts are come out with wings—a numerous race of sectaries and heretics, who have renewed all the old heresies, and invented monstrous opinions of their own. These have filled our cities, villages, camps, houses— nay, our churches and pulpits, too, and lead the poor deluded people with them to the pit of perdition." Doubtless the poor Bishop, being a self-complacent Anglican, failed to perceive that he himself was as much of a deluded sectary and heretic as any of them. It was not till 1582 that a Catholic New Testament appeared, and that was not in England, but in France, at Rheims, where a colony of persecuted Catholics had fled, including Cardinal Allen, Gregory Martin and Robert Bristow, who were mainly responsible for this new translation. William Allen, formerly Canon of York, later Archbishop of Mechlin, and lastly Cardinal, had founded a college at Douay for the training of priests for the English mission in 1568. He was compelled to remove it to Rheims in 1578 owing to Huguenot riots; and there, as I said, in 1582 they issued the New Testament in English for Catholics. It was a translation, of course, from the Latin Vulgate, which had been declared by the Council of Trent to be the authorized text of Scripture for the Church. Martin was the principal translator, while Bristow mainly contributed the notes, which are powerful and illuminative. The whole was intended to be of service both to priests and people, to give them a true and sound rendering of the original writings, to save them from the numberless false and incorrect versions in circulation, and to provide them with something wherewith to refute the heretics who then, as ever, approached with a text in their mouth.

(2) Needless to say, the appearance of this New Testament, with its annotations, at once aroused the fiercest opposition. Queen Elizabeth ordered the searchers to seek out and confiscate every copy they could find. If a priest was found in possession of it, he was forthwith imprisoned. Torture by rack was applied to those who circulated it, and a scholar, Dr. Fulke, was appointed to refute it. All these measures, be it noted, kind reader, were taken by parties who advocated loudly the unlimited right of private judgment. In 1593 the College returned to Douay, and there in 1609 the Old Testament was added, and the Catholic Bible in English was complete, and is called the Douay Bible [or the Douay-Rheims Bible]. "Complete" we may well call it; it is the only really complete Bible in English [as of 1911], for it contains those seven books of the Old Testament which I pointed out before were, and are, omitted by the Protestants in their editions. So that we can claim to have not only the pure, unadulterated Bible, but the whole of it, without addition or subtraction: a translation of the Vulgate, which is itself the work of St. Jerome in the

fourth century, which, again, is the most authoritative and correct of all the early copies of Holy Scripture. At a single leap we thus arrive at that great work, completed by the greatest scholar of his day, who had access to manuscripts and authorities that have now perished, and who, living so near the days of the Apostles, and, as it were, close to the very fountainhead, was able to produce a copy of the inspired writings which, for correctness, can never be equalled.

We may feel justly proud of our Douay Bible. We need not declare it to be perfect in all respects, either in regard to its English style or its employment of words from foreign languages; we need not feel the less affection or admiration for it though we should suggest the possibility of revision and improvement in some particulars—it has, indeed, been re-edited and revised ere now, especially by Bishop Challoner. But when all is said and done, it is a noble version with a noble history: true, honest, scholarly, faithful to the original. The Catholic Church has nothing to regret in her policy or her action toward English versions of the Scriptures. She has not issued one version one year and cancelled it the next because of its corruptions and errors, its partisan notes, or political doctrines. Nobly she has stood for reverence and caution in respect of translating God's Holy Word into the vulgar tongue. She was slow in acting, I admit, if by slowness we mean deliberation and prudence, for she saw with unerring vision the evils that were certain to result from a hasty casting of pearls before swine. But when she did act, she acted decisively and once for all. Who is there that has followed the sad story of the non-Catholic treatment of the Sacred Scriptures but will be forced by contrast to admire the wisdom, the calm dignity, the consistent and deliberate policy of the Ecclesiastical authorities of the Catholic Church in England, which stands as a reproof to the violent, blundering, malicious methods of the sectaries and which, if it had been acquiesced in by others, would have saved the Word of God from infinite degradation and contempt?

(3) Hatred against her version of the Bible when it first appeared was so deep that an oath sworn on it was not deemed to be valid. It was on this sacred volume that Mary, Queen of Scots, laid her hand and swore her innocence the night before her execution. The Earl of Kent at once interposed with the remark that the Book was a Popish and false translation, and in consequence the oath was of no value. "Does your Lordship suppose," was the quiet answer of the noble Queen, "that my oath would be the better if I swore on *your* translation, which I do *not* believe?" Thanks be to God, the Douay version has now so established its position, and hatred to it and to its authors has so diminished, that a Catholic may, even in these lands, swear upon it in conscience, and his word is believed as any other man's in a Court of Law. Found in thousands of pious Catholic homes at the present

hour, we may comfort ourselves with the reflection that, in this kingdom, there has now for long existed the true version of the Gospel of our Blessed Lord and the inspired words of His holy Apostles and Evangelists, as they have been handed down and preserved by the Catholic Church from the beginning, unchangeable and unchanged; and we may feel the most absolute certainty that, as it is the true version, so, at a date not incalculably distant, it will prove to be the only one, for the others will have gone to join their predecessors, and been consigned to a happy oblivion, and only survive in the memory of him who glances at their musty covers and faded pages beneath the glass cases of library or museum.

～16～

Envoy

AND now my task is finished, and you, dear reader, if you have followed it up, will utter, I am sure, a hearty *Deo gratias!* As sincerely and as clearly as possible, I have tried to show that it is to the Catholic Church under God that we owe the preservation and integrity of the Sacred Scriptures. The Old Testament she took over from the Jewish Church; to it she added the New Testament, the work of her own Apostles and Bishops; and comprising them in one great whole, declared that they had the Holy Ghost for their author, and were neither to be increased nor diminished. Throughout the ages, when there was no other Church, she has preserved them from error, saved them from destruction, multiplied them in every language under Heaven and put them with the necessary prudence in her people's hands. Again and again heretics and apostates have tried to mutilate and corrupt them—indeed, have actually done so; but the Roman Church has ever preserved a version pure and entire. She claims that she alone knows the meaning of their teaching, and alone possesses the right to interpret them to men. She will tolerate no tampering with the sacred text, and in these days especially, when scientists and critics who have lost belief in the supernatural attack them and labor to overthrow their Divine authority and authorship, Rome alone stands as their protector; to her alone pious lovers of the Sacred Volume, be they Catholic or Protestant, must look to save it and defend it. The Pope has appointed a standing Biblical Commission to guard the integrity and authenticity of Holy Scripture. This is but natural; for he stands as it were *in loco parentis*; the Bible is the Church's offspring. But it is surely the keenest irony of history that, while Protestants themselves are striving with might and main to pull to pieces the ancient object of their veneration, the Catholic Church, ever reputed its deadliest enemy, alone is left of all Christian bodies to save it from destruction. And this she will do, as she has ever done in the past; it is part of her office in this world; there is no other that has either the right or the power to do it. If the Bible loses its sovereign place in the heart and mind of non-Catholics, as it is rapidly doing, it is the work of those who, whether in Germany, or Britain or America, have loudly professed themselves its greatest champions.

The Catholic Church, on the other hand, in her long history has nothing to be ashamed of in her treatment of it, but deserves the praise and thanks of all Christians for so zealously and fearlessly protecting it from corruption and contempt. Indeed, I will say that a simple study of her attitude toward the inspired Scriptures, in comparison with that of all heretical bodies, will furnish one of the strongest arguments that she is the True Church of Christ.

Venerable and inspired as Catholics regard the Bible, great as is their devotion to it for spiritual reading and support of doctrine, we yet do not pretend to lean upon it alone as the Rule of faith and morals. Along with it we take that great Word that was never written, Tradition, and hold by both the one and the other interpreted by the living voice of the Catholic Church speaking through her Supreme Head, the infallible Vicar of Christ. Here we have a Guide that has never failed, and never can, in teaching us our duty both to God and man. Not on the quicksands of human and varying judgment, but on the Rock of Divine Authority, we place our feet; and, amidst the warring of opinions and the conflict of numberless editions and versions of Sacred Scripture, and the confused and contradictory interpretations of texts, we find an unassailable refuge in the decision of Rome; and in submitting to the judgment of that Church to which Christ gave Divine authority to teach when He said, "Go ye and teach all nations," we find a sure consolation and an abiding peace.

Individual interpretation of the Bible—the most sublime but also the most difficult Book ever penned—can never bring satisfaction, can never give infallible certainty, can never place a man in possession of that great objective body of truth which Our Blessed Lord taught, and which it is necessary to salvation that all should believe. The experience of many centuries proves it. It can not do so because it was never meant to do so. It produces not unity, but division; not peace, but strife. Only listening to those to whom Jesus Christ said, "He that heareth you heareth Me," only sinking his own fads and fancies and submitting with childlike confidence to those whom the Redeemer sent out to teach in His Name and with His authority—only this, I say, will satisfy a man, and give to his intellect repose, and to his soul a "peace that surpasseth all understanding." Then no longer will he be tormented with contentious disputings about this passage of the Bible and that, no longer racked and rent and "tossed to and fro with every wind of doctrine," changing with the changing years. He will, on the contrary, experience a joy and comfort and certainty that nothing can shake in being able to say, "O my God, I believe whatever Thy Holy Catholic Church believes and teaches, because Thou hast revealed it, Who canst neither deceive nor be deceived." God grant that many Bible readers and Bible lovers may obtain the grace to make this act of faith, and pass from an unreasoning subservience to a Book to reasonable obedience and submission to its maker and defender—the Catholic and Roman Church.

Bibliographical Note

Catholic

The Bible and the Rule of Faith. Abbé Bégin.
The Bible: Its Use and Abuse. Paul McLachlan.
Concerning the Holy Bible. J. S. Vaughan.
Text-Books of Catholic Theology. Tanquerey,
    Hunter, etc.
Catholic Dictionary, Catholic Cyclopædia.
C.T.S. [Catholic Truth Society] publications. Clarke,
    Anderson, Donnelly, M. C. L., Allnatt, etc.
The Question Box, Faith of Our Fathers, etc.
Introduction to Old Testament and New Testament.
    Cornely.
The Old English Bible. Gasquet.
Catholic Students' "Aids" to the Study of the Bible.
    H. Pope, O. P.

Protestant

English Church Histories. Dixon, Hook, Blunt.
The Bible and the Church. Westcott.
The Dark Ages. Maitland.
History of the English Bible. Burnett Thompson.
The English Bible. Milligan.
How the Bible Came to Us. Herne.
English Bibles. Doré.
Our Bible. Talbot.
How We Got Our Bible. Smyth.
Introduction to New Testament Criticism. Scrivener.
Helps to Study of the Bible. (Oxford).
The Bibles of England. Edgar.
Our English Bible. Hoare.